# FULCANELLI

Patrick Rivière

# FULCANELLI
His True Identity Revealed
Light On His Work

Translation by Micheline Deschreider

Red Pill Press
2009

Originally published in French as *Fulcanelli, Sa veritable identité enfin révélée, La lumière sur son oeuvre*, by Editions de Vecchi S.A., Paris, 2000.

The author thanks the following people: my friend Gérard de Santis, for his willingness to carefully undertake tasks in my name; to the archivists at the Academy of Sciences and of the Conservatory of Arts and Métiers for their kind diligence.

Second English Edition
© Patrick Rivière

ISBN 987-1-897244-44-9

All rights reserved. No part of this publication may be reproduced, stored in a retrieval system, or transmitted, in any form or by any means, electronic, mechanical, photocopying, recording, or otherwise, without the written prior permission of the author.

Printed in Poland

*In posthumous tribute to Eugène Canseliet,
Our good Master in Savignies…*

# TABLE OF CONTENTS

| | |
|---|---:|
| INTRODUCTION | 11 |
| **I. ALCHEMY IN PARIS AT THE BEGINNING OF THE TWENTIETH CENTURY** | 13 |
| **Marcellin Berthelot** | 14 |
| **Albert Poisson** | 15 |
| **Alchemical Gold** | 17 |
| **Potable Gold** | 19 |
| **Scientific Discoveries** | 20 |
| **Pierre Dujols, alias Magophon** | 21 |
| **Cyliani, *Hermes Unveiled*** | 23 |
| **Irène Hillel-Erlanger, *Voyages en Kadéidoscope*** | 23 |
| **II. THE ALCHEMICAL *MYSTERY OF THE CATHEDRALS*** | 31 |
| **Fragments from the Preface by Eugène Canseliet** | 31 |
| **The Mystery of the Cathedrals** | 32 |
|    The Origins of Gothic Art | 32 |
|    Interpretation of the Imagery | 34 |
|    Alchemical Symbolism | 36 |
| **III. *DWELLINGS OF THE PHILOSOPHERS*** | 39 |
| **Volume One** | 39 |
| **Second Volume** | 43 |
| **Did Fulcanelli have a master?** | 46 |

| | |
|---|---:|
| **IV. THE LEGENDARY ENCOUNTER BETWEEN FULCANELLI AND EUGÈNE CANSELIET** | 49 |
| **The Legendary Encounter** | 50 |
| **Close to the Athanor** | 54 |
| **Fulcanelli's Manuscripts** | 59 |
| **Evidence of the Precise Year of Fulcanelli's Disappearance** | 61 |
|     Some Apparently Contradictory Statements | 61 |
|     Evidence for the Actual Year of Fulcanelli's Departure | 63 |
| **V. WHO WAS JEAN-JULIEN CHAMPAGNE?** | 67 |
| **Memorable Meetings** | 68 |
| **Strange Company** | 74 |
| **Julien Champagne Poses as Fulcanelli** | 78 |
| **The Much-Debated Identity of Fulcanelli** | 83 |
|     Erroneous Hypotheses | 83 |
|     Geneviève Dubois' Regrettable Misconception | 88 |
| **A Monument to Subjectivity** | 91 |
| **VI. THESE MEN OF THE INSTITUTE AND ALCHEMY** | 93 |
| **Was Fulcanelli a Famous Scientist?** | 94 |
| **The Mysterious "Mr Violette"** | 100 |
| **VII. THE MASTER'S "COAT OF ARMS"** | 105 |
| **VIII. WHERE THE MASTER'S IDENTITY FINDS THE LIGHT OF DAY** | 109 |
| **"The Fire of the Sun" and Solar Radiation** | 111 |
| **Dumas, Berthelot, Lesseps and… "High Temperatures"** | 120 |
| **From High Temperatures to "Thermo-Master"** | 124 |
| **The Light Standard and Accumulated Evidence** | 125 |

| | |
|---|---|
| IX. THE PARISIAN CAREER OF THE SAVANT | 133 |
| **Les Arts et Métiers** | **134** |
| X. FROM THE MASTER'S SUCCESSION TO THE "STRANGE MANOR" | 145 |
| XI. *FINIS GLORIAE MUNDI* THE END OF THE GLORY OF THE WORLD | 155 |
| **The Reign of Man** | **159** |
| **The Deluge** | **159** |
| **Atlantis** | **160** |
| **The Burning** | **162** |
| **The Golden Age** | **163** |
| **The Cyclic Cross of Hendaye** | **164** |
| **Regarding a Forged *Finis Gloriae Mundi*** | **169** |
| XII. EUGÈNE CANSELIET'S ALCHEMICAL MEMOIRS | 177 |
| APPENDIX | 185 |
| LETTER ADDRESSED TO FULCANELLI'S "INITIATOR" AFTER HIS ACCESS TO ADEPTSHIP | 187 |
| BIBLIOGRAPHY | 191 |

# Introduction

Who was the enigmatic alchemist of the last century known only to the public by the pseudonym of Fulcanelli? What was his actual identity?

Attempting to unveil the *inviolable* by disclosing the answer to this question is the heavy task that seems, by compelling events, to have fallen to me at the dawn of this third millennium. It am undertaking this task, even though I still have some qualms about deeming myself any more authorized to do this today than I was in the past!

Why do I submit yet another study on the subject of Fulcanelli and insist on his identity, the truth of which I discovered nearly twenty years ago? What is the underlying reason for this disclosure? In short, after a long period of hesitancy lasting no less than three lustrums[1], I think that the moment seems appropriate to shed light on the true personality of the greatest alchemist of our time, a man who enraptured my adolescent dreams and to whose erudition I have never ceased to be subservient over the course of many years.

My disclosure is encouraged by the renewed and increasing interest of *truth seekers* who are eager to clear up the mystery that surrounded the actual identity of a character whose will it was that his anonymity be preserved in the last century of the second millennium. However, it is primarily because I also see arising in the world of publishers, as well as on the *Web*, endless hypotheses that do not at all - and this is a euphemism - reflect the benevolent neutrality befitting such an endeavour as divulging the identity of Fulcanelli! Such a disclosure becomes particularly necessary when

---

[1] A period of five years. (Tr.)

certain writers question the moral integrity and honesty of Eugène Canseliet, the only disciple of the said Fulcanelli, in contempt of any historical objectivity and, even worse I think, of the respect due to the memory of the man who, for his entire life, faithfully preserved the message bequeathed to him by his Master as a sacred trust.

For the present purposes, a meticulous and concise investigation is necessary, the thread of which I am going to try and confide to my readers in the lines that follow. I submitted this information as an *avant-première* to my friend Johan Dreue who, with my permission, took up some of the themes on his Internet site and on the CD-ROM he was then preparing. May the readers of these lines forgive me if I repeat myself, but I solved the *Fulcanelli enigma* almost twenty years ago.

In this first English edition of my work, new material has been added, for since the first publication in French in 2000 (*Fulcanelli, sa véritable identité révélée*,[2] éd. De Vecchi), certain facts, new evidence and actual documents have been discovered that have confirmed what some of my readers had, at the time of the first publication in 2000, considered to be a gratuitous assumption! This evidence is to be added to the "Fulcanelli file" and represents, as readers will realize for themselves, major and henceforth undeniable evidence for my identification.

I have also added for this edition a section on the interpretation of Fulcanelli and his work by certain American authors who have projected their own fantasies onto a work whose depth they clearly can neither appreciate nor understand.

---

[2] *Fulcanelli: His True Identity Revealed* (Tr.).

# I
# Alchemy in Paris at the Beginning of the Twentieth Century

The end of the 19th century saw a renewed interest in Alchemy, the ancient "Science of Hermes", thanks to scientific discoveries at the time in the field of isomeric[3] varieties of so-called "compound" bodies. It was discovered that "simple" allotropic[4] elements such as carbon shared a similar chemical composition with a diamond or a piece of graphite, even if these bodies were quite dissimilar in appearance! The problem of the alchemical transmutation of metals, for so long the dream of the "gold-making" alchemists, was resurfacing. Jean-Baptiste Dumas wrote on this subject in his *Leçons sur la philosophie chimique*[5]:

> Can we be permitted to admit the existence of isomeric simple bodies? This question is closely linked to the transmutation of metal. If the answer is affirmative, then it would mean that the possibility exists for a successful outcome of the search for the philosopher's stone... Thus it is necessary to refer to experience, and experience, it must be said, has not, up to this point, contradicted the possibility of transmuting simple elements/bodies... Given the current level of our knowledge, this idea cannot be considered an absurdity.

---

[3] In chemistry, isomers are molecules with the same chemical formula and often with the same kinds of bonds between atoms, but in which the atoms are arranged differently. Many isomers share similar if not identical properties in most chemical contexts.
[4] Allotropy (Gr. *allos*, other, and *tropos*, manner), a name applied by Jöns Jakob Berzelius to the property possessed by certain substances of existing in forms with different chemical structures; the various forms are known as allotropes. Jöns Jakob Berzelius used the name in an entirely different sense (see *Macmillan Encyclopedia of Chemistry*, edited by J.J.Lagowski, 1997, Simon Schuster).
[5] *Lessons on Chemical Philosophy* (Tr.).

*Marcellin Bertholet*

## Marcellin Berthelot

The learned chemist, Marcellin Berthelot, who dedicated more than twenty years to the laborious study of original alchemical texts in Greek and Arabic, reported the results of his works in three well-documented books entitled: *Les Origines de l'Alchimie*[6] (Paris, 1885), *Introduction à l'étude de la chimie des Anciens et du Moyen Âge*[7] (Paris, 1889) and, in collaboration with Ruelle, *Collection des anciens alchimistes grecs*[8] (Paris, 1887). His son, Daniel Berthelot, stated in a monograph published in 1895 entitled, *L'Allotropie des corps simples*[9] – allotropy being isomerism in "simple" bodies – that

---

[6] *The Origins of Alchemy* (Tr.).
[7] *Introduction to the Study of the Chemistry of the Ancients and of the Middle Ages* (Tr.).
[8] *Collection of the Ancient Greek Alchemists* (Tr.).
[9] *The Allotropy of Simple Bodie* (Tr.)s.

this notion naturally brought up the question of the unity of matter, a principle that was supported by mainstream science, although it had already been evoked time and again by the ancient alchemists throughout their writings. Like his eminent predecessors of old, Dom Pernéty wrote:

*Matter is one and every thing, so say the philosophers, because it is the radical principle of every combined thing. It is in all things and similar to all things because it is likely [to adopt] any form, although it does so prior to its being specified into any individual species of the three realms of Nature.*[10]

## Albert Poisson

In 1891, young Albert Poisson wrote in his very erudite book entitled, *Théorie et symboles des alchimistes* (Éditions Traditionnelles, Chacornac, Paris, 1891)[11]:

At the foundation of hermetic theory we find a great Law: the Unity of Matter. Matter is One, but it can assume various forms, and, in these novel forms, combine itself to itself and produce new bodies in indefinite numbers. This first matter was called 'seed', 'chaos', 'universal substance'.

The case of Albert Poisson is quite interesting. As an adolescent, he was already engrossed in alchemy. He haunted the shops along the banks of the River Seine in search of ancient hermetic manuscripts, and paid daily visits to the *Bibliothèque Nationale* and the *Bibliothèque de l'Arsenal* to peruse the alchemical treatises that were kept in their old stacks. He spent the rest of his time collecting the equipment he needed - retorts, furnaces, crucibles, coal, etc. - in the small laboratory he installed in his room on the rue Saint-Denis. Although totally devoured by his passion, he had also undertaken the study of medicine. At the age of twenty-three, the young student published three remarkable essays on the elaboration of the Great Work: *Théorie et symboles des alchimistes* (quoted above), the French translation of five alchemical treatises from the pens of the

---

[10] *Greek and Egyptian Fables Unveiled* (Tr.).
[11] *Theory and Symbols of the Alchemists* (Tr.).

greatest hermetic philosophers: Arnauld de Villeneuve, Raymond Lulle, Albert le Grand, Roger Bacon, and Paracelsus, and also in the same year, an essay entitled, *Nicolas Flamel et l'alchimie au XIV$^e$ siècle*[12] (Éditions Traditionnelles, Chacornac). In addition to this, he published a number of articles in the magazine *Le Voile d'Isis*[13], under the 'nom de plume' of *Philophotes*.

*Albert Poisson*
*1865-1894*

His actual master in alchemy is assumed to have been Rémi Pierret, a shoemaker by trade and caretaker of the premises at 12, Passage Ménilmontant. A Mason with a passion for hermetism, it is believed that he authored, among other texts, an alchemical compendium on processes involving dew and leading to *potable gold*, inspired by a manuscript written in 1744. Since the bookcases in his modest lodgings were richly stocked with alchemical documents, and he received visits there from Albert Poisson,

---

[12] *Nicolas Flamel and Alchemy in the 14th Century* (Tr.).

[13] *The Veil of Isis* (Tr.).

Stanislas de Guaïta, Marc-Haven, Papus and Victor-Emile Michelet, we must ask the question: did he labour in secret in the laboratory? The fact is that he discreetly *disappeared* once his pupil was on the right track.

Sadly, not yet twenty-five years of age - totally consumed by the alchemical fire and overwhelmed by inadequately-treated phthisis[14], which was compounded by over-exhaustion and under-nourishment - the young and brilliant disciple of Hermes died on a Sunday morning in 1893 after a long bout of coughing and a violent fever, leaving to posterity the fruit of his published studies.

**Alchemical Gold**

The sad destiny of the lamented Albert Poisson should not make us oblivious to the other names linked to this renewed interest in the Ancient Science of Hermes. To begin with, there is François Jollivet-Castelot and his "hyperchemical" movement, created around 1895 with the *Association alchimique de France,* of which *L'Hyperchimie* was the official journal :

> A. Poisson has revealed the secrets of the Ancient Masters.
> The aim of the director of *L'Hyperchimie* was and still is to adapt them to contemporary theories that should confirm the truths perceived by the Egyptian hierophants in their sanctuaries.

Thus was defined the ambitious program of that more *"archemical"* than *"alchemical"* association that gave birth to a genuine school located in Douai. This was the context in which old Tiffereau expressed himself. In 1889, he published *L'Or et la transmutation des métaux*[15], a work in which he described the result of his first transmutation, obtained in 1842 while he was travelling in Mexico (Guadalajara). Here is the process as he recounted it:

> After having exposed some pure nitric acid to the action of the sun's rays for two days, I then added to it some pure silver filings that were alloyed with copper in the same proportion as coin alloy. A strong reaction manifested, accompanied by a copious release of nitrous gas.

---

[14] Consumption or pulmonary tuberculosis. (Tr.)
[15] *Gold and the Transmutation of Meta* (Tr.)

The liquor, left to rest, revealed an abundant settling of intact, mass-agglomerated filings.

I left the liquid unattended for twelve days while a continuous nitrous-gas release took place, and I noticed that the agglomerated settling had significantly increased in volume. I then added a little water to the dissolution without any precipitate occurring, and I again left the liquor to rest for five days. Meanwhile, new vapours continued to be released.

At the end of these five days, I heated the liquor to boiling point and kept it there until the release of nitrous vapours ceased; after which, I let it dry off.

The substance obtained by desiccation was dry, dull, and blackish green. There was no appearance of crystallisation, and no saline deposits.

Then, having treated this substance with pure, boiling nitric acid for ten hours, I saw the substance become bright green, and it continued to aggregate in small masses. I added a new quantity of pure, concentrated acid, and again brought it to a boil. It was at that moment that, at last, I saw the disaggregated substance acquire the brightness of natural gold.

I collected this product, and relinquished a large quantity of it to a series of tests in order to compare it to pure, natural gold. I was unable to observe the slightest difference between natural gold and the artificial gold I had just obtained. [...]

Such is, Gentlemen, in all truthfulness, the achievement obtained, the constant results of which I was able to reproduce several times in Mexico.

However, I was unable to reproduce this same achievement *when in France*, and when dealing with *more significant quantities*. Doubtlessly, I erroneously assessed the causes that act in the reactions, by virtue of which metals, soluble in nitric acid, become insoluble when constituting themselves in a particular molecular state, which results in properties entirely different from the ones those same metals possessed before having undergone those reactions.

Should these changes, to which the *action of the sunlight* seems to contribute so potently, be attributed to a special electric or magnetic state, or to the part played by nitrogen under this influence?

The above text became the subject of a memorandum presented at the *Académie des Sciences* on May 8, 1854 - a text that was studied intently by Eugène Chevreul and J.B. Dumas, in particular.

## Potable Gold

Even the great Swedish playwright, Auguste Strindberg, showed some interest in the *École hyperchimique* of F. Jollivet-Castelot. In 1896, he sent Jollivet-Castelot reports of his personal discoveries regarding "transmutation into gold". The two men became friends, both being convinced that they had succeeded in artificially obtaining the precious metal in infinitesimal quantities. Jollivet-Castelot even went so far as to claim that he had succeeded in producing a genuine "potable gold" endowed with eminently therapeutic virtues, since it was, according to him, nothing less than the *Elixir of Life* of the Ancients!

As for Dr Alphonse Jobert, he feverishly sought contacts with François Jollivet-Castelot, and reproached the latter for deviating from the hermetic Tradition in favour of *archemical* manipulations of a purely chemical nature. He himself claimed to have obtained successful transmutations into gold and silver, and allegedly demonstrated this publicly in Paris in 1905. Jobert was vastly cultured and well educated. He was a medical doctor, had received a master's degree from the *École des Mines,* and seemed to possess a certain knowledge of old alchemical texts. He wrote alchemical instructions in the form of notes that one of his pupils, René Schwaeblé, appropriated and published under his own name under the title, *Alchimie simplifiée*[16].

Alphonse Jobert (alias Dousson), even went so far as to provocatively claim that, on the condition of being provided an adequate laboratory, he would be able to supply the French State a mass of precious metal of no less than thirty billion gold-francs! Of course, nothing came of it, and early one morning in 1913, Dr Jobert left his lodgings on rue Rosalie (or Marie-Rose) at Closerie des Lilas, and was *never seen again.*

---

[16] *Alchemy Simplified* (Tr.) Librairie du Magnétisme, Paris

## Scientific Discoveries

On the purely scientific plane, discoveries made by Henri Becquerel in 1896 regarding the radioactivity of uranium salts completely modified the status of physio-chemical knowledge of the time. In addition, Pierre and Marie Curie, via their own remarkable work in 1898, succeeded in isolating radium, which they had laboriously extracted from pitchblende. As uranium produces radium on its own through radioactive transformation, this opened up a horizon of new prospects for those interested in transmutory alchemy at the beginning of the twentieth century. This was, in a certain fashion, scientific acknowledgement of the merits of the principle of the *transmutation* of matter. The old dream of alchemists throughout the ages, a 'chimerical' art for many, had at last become a reality! The 'simple-body' allotropy explanation was relegated to the background, and the problematic now shifted to the level of the atom, its nucleus, and its electron configuration.

In this "alchemic-scientific" context, a book was published at the start of the first World War that paradoxically renewed the links to the alchemical Tradition of the Ancients. It was the commentary of a certain Magophon who, in his *Hypotypose,* undertook to describe and clarify the various phases of the Great Work as evoked in the famous book of 1702, illustrated by J. J. Manget, a book which was already known in its first edition (de La Rochelle, 1677) as the alchemists' "mute Bible" since it only contained illustrated plates. This book was indeed the famous *Mutus Liber,* signed by a certain *Altus*, whose real name was either Jacob Sulat (anagram of *Altus*) or, more likely, Tollé. The printing of the clarification of the "picture book without words" by the *Librairie Nourry*, Paris $5^{th}$, in 1914 was limited to 285 (numbered) copies. Who was the mysterious author of the comments who hid behind the pseudonym of "Magophon" (literally, "the voice of the magus")?

It was a secret to no one. The author was a bookseller named Pierre Dujols, aged 52, whose first peculiarity was that he was a descendant of the Valois branch of the French royal family. This was a subject his elder brother, Antoine Dujols de Valois, had written on in an essay published in Marseilles in 1879 - an essay that had elicited reactions in the local press. The title was *Valois contre Bourbons*[17] and the sub-title: *Simples éclaircissements avec pièces justificatives*[18], was signed: "a scion of Valois stock ".

## Pierre Dujols, alias Magophon

Pierre Dujols had a bookshop in the 6th district of Paris called the *Librairie du Merveilleux*[19] at 76, rue de Rennes. It had quite a program! In addition to publishing a magazine created by René Guénon called *La Gnose (Gnosis)*, all the occult groups of the time assiduously visited the famous bookshop run by Dujols and his assistant, A. Thomas, a man as addicted to esoterism as his employer. Within the walls of the *Librairie du Merveilleux*, lovers of the occult rubbed elbows with magicians, kabbalists, hermetists and, of course, more or less *operative* alchemists. The scholarly bookseller increasingly advocated the *phonetic Cabala*, which was, in his opinion, the "green language of the birds", a form of word play that - with knowledge of ancient Greek - permitted one to decipher many an arcane document. In this undertaking, which at first glance seemed to be his own, he relied upon the works of the archaeologist and philologist, Grasset d'Orcet (b. 1828), that were published in *Revue Britannique*. These works (to which we shall return later on) recommended a deciphering method used by the ancient trade-guilds that was based upon phonetic assonance, like a hermetic Kabbala.

In addition, Pierre Dujols and his wife received numerous friends who were specialists in esoterism at their salon in the 5th district, located on rue Henri-Barbusse (formerly rue Denfert-Rochereau). Among these was the kabbalist, Paul Vulliaud, who shared Pierre Dujols's interest for this other *Cabala,* which although merely phonetic, also contained undeniable esoteric teachings. Also attending these fruitful meetings was a discreet alchemist by the name of Louis Faugeron. Faugeron practised the hermetic art following the directives of his master, Pierre Dujols, and spent his whole life in quest of the *Philosophers' Stone*.

---

[17] *Valois vs. Bourbons* (Tr.).
[18] *Simple explanations with supporting documents*. (Tr.)
[19] Bookshop of Wonders. (Tr.)

*Pierre Dujols de Valois*

Here is how Magophon - alias Pierre Dujols – introduced his memorable, alchemical *Hypotypose*:

> By clipping these few pages of comments to the allegorical plates of the *Mutus Liber*, we undertook, without taking off the philosopher's cloak [*i.e. in a veiled manner - note by PR*], to make their reading easier by way of a sincere interpretation, as true, patient, scientific researchers labouring in the manner of industrious bees, and not as frivolous, idle amateurs who spend their lives uselessly fluttering about from book to book without ever stopping at any one in order to extract from it the mellifluous substance…

To the question once asked by his friend Paul Le Cour, (founder of the *Atlantis* association), who considered alchemy as merely an inner and spiritual quest, he answered without hesitation that Le Cour was "entirely mistaken" and that

> …intellectual hermetism could not be understood without working on material bodies, and that hermetic terminology could not be related to scientific terminology".

## Cyliani, *Hermes Unveiled*

In 1915, a very odd small work entitled *Hermès dévoilé*[20], "dedicated to posterity" and written under the pseudonym Cyliani (referring to Mount Cyllène, dedicated to Mercury), was republished by *Éditions Traditionnelles*, Chacornac, quai Saint-Michel, which is located very close to Notre-Dame. The first edition had been published in 1832. The author's poignant tale, expressed in the romantic style of the time, is bestowed with a particularly moving quality. The foreword begins:

> The Heavens having allowed me to succeed in achieving the philosopher's stone after thirty-seven years spent in its quest - staying awake at least fifteen hundred nights, and passing through innumerable misfortunes and irreparable losses - I believed I could offer to Youth, the hope of its country, the heart-rending picture of my life to serve as a lesson and to turn it away from an art that shows at first glance the most pleasant-looking white and red roses that are actually prickly with thorns, and of which the path leading to the place where they can be culled is full of dangers.

> As the universal medicine is a boon more precious than the gift of riches, its knowledge is naturally imparted on studious men who think that they are happier than a multitude of persons. This is the reason that prompted me to transmit to posterity the operations to be carried out, in the greatest detail, without omitting anything, and to also prevent the ruin of honest people and be of service to a suffering mankind ...

## Irène Hillel-Erlanger, *Voyages en Kadéidoscope*

In the autumn of 1919, Editions Georges Crès in Paris published a rather amazing book. It was amazing firstly due to its *Dadaist* style; *Dada* being an 'avant-garde' movement founded by Tristan Tzara, a forerunner of Surrealism. The setting of the book, all in a very *modern style,* was evocative of jazz-bands, Cubism and the obsolete charm of the bars in Saint-Germain-des-Prés and Montparnasse. Secondly, and mainly, it was amazing because of its content, which undeniably unveiled the operations of the alchemical

---

[20] *Hermes Unveiled*. (Tr.)

Great Work, until then kept secret. The title was *Voyages en Kaléidoscope*[21], and it was penned by Irène Hillel-Erlanger.

A member of the entourage of the poet Louis Aragon, the author was a young woman already known in literary circles for a previous novel, *Stances, Sonnets et Chansons*[22], published by Grasset under the meaningful pseudonym of Claude Lorrey (*l'or y est*[23]!). Certainly, the title and the only illustration - a thermometer, which was designed by Master Van Dongen himself - did not fail to astonish readers! And what an astounding tale it was. The tale of an inventor named Joël Joze who, thanks to his weird "kaleidoscope", wiles away the time bringing out into the open that which, in essence, had remained occult. Two irremediably different women

---

[21] *Journeys in a Kaleidoscope.* (Tr.)
[22] *Stanzas, Sonnets, and Songs.* (Tr.)
[23] *The gold is there.* (Tr.)

exert an immense fascination upon him: *Grâce,* who, of course, is grace and wisdom incarnate, while *Véra* appears venal and fiendish. Gilly, the faithful assistant of the brilliant inventor, helps his master achieve the much hoped for success. Here is how the author depicts the characters in her book:

> Joël Joze: Superior mankind (so little), alternately Seeing and Blind.
>
> Grâce: Grace (naturally).
>
> Véra: Voluptuousness. Perfect form of ferocious Pleasure.
>
> Seemingly opposites, Grâce and Véra are essentially closely related; or better: the same Person under two Aspects. Véra relies on Sensation, Grâce relies on Truth. When one or the other increases, it is to the detriment of the other, and to the jeopardy of mankind. A double emanation of the Unknowable, such as Time and Eternity, Divine Necessity and human Freedom; this, undoubtedly, we shall understand a little better when on another Plane.
>
> As for Gilly, for us he is "the salt of the Earth" - exactly: the faithful Servant.

Further on in the text we read the following paragraph, eloquent in its hermetic preoccupations:

> A Palm grove in the middle of Paris... At the centre of the Palm Grove, a fountain-head flowing in a white-marble basin ... The Rejuvenating One? Joël Joze remembers. In his youth, he had heard people talking about this quasi-miraculous Fountain. It healed, so it was said, nerve and eye ailments. Too simple a remedy. A common name. Chemistry has changed that. But do some people treat themselves with the Rejuvenating One?... Still, when all passes and returns, why wonder? If one acquires the habit of thinking about the mystery of things - if, to some extent, one gets into the habit of probing the Occult, one clearly realises that everything transforms, acts, influences in reciprocity, depending upon the Atmosphere, which continually modifies itself at every moment ...

Furthermore, it is to be noted that if the extravagant Countess Véra, purely a product of the *Belle Epoque,* lives on avenue Montaigne (former Allée des Veuves[24]), her sister Grâce, always veiled, lives

---

[24] Widows' Lane. (Tr.)

not very far from her. From this, we are only one step removed from concluding that the said *Palm grove* may have been the Moresque or Egyptian Pavilion belonging to the prestigious de Lesseps family, at no. 22 - the latter residing at no. 11 of said avenue - although this is a step we shall be wary of taking too hastily. Surely, however, it is at least troubling that Irène Hillel-Erlanger frequented the de Lesseps' town-house. This is a point that we shall come back to later.

As to the thermometer - let us not forget that it was designed by the master-painter Van Dongen. The book was literally a "thermo-master"[25] since it revealed the temperature scale of the Great Work.

Irène Hillel-Erlanger came from a family of wealthy bankers, the De Camondos, that owned a town-house that is now a museum. One of the young woman's grandfathers, Count Abraham de Camondo, who died in 1873, was the banker to the Sultan of Constantinople. Isaac de Camondo was a philanthropist who had gathered around him many artists, such as the musician, Paul Dukas. It was also rumoured at the time that Irène's father was subsidising the works of an unknown alchemist. Regarding her private life, after an unhappy and painful love affair, Irène married a renowned musician of the Opéra Comique, Camille Erlanger, (awarded the Prix de Rome, or "Rome Prize", in 1888). The couple lived behind the Arch de Triomphe on the rue du Commandant Marchand. Their Parisian salon was attended by the best company.

On the night of a sumptuous cocktail party organized for the publication of her book, Irène Hillel-Erlanger contracted food-poisoning after eating oysters at dinner. She is supposed to have died in mysterious circumstances several weeks later, in 1920. Did someone attempt to poison her for having revealed high-calibre, alchemical secrets? The fact is that during the week following the cocktail party, all copies of the book were confiscated and pulped; only a very few copies escaped that fate and ended up in bookstalls on the banks of the River Seine. Then, rumour had it that a financial trust or a group of international gold smugglers had had Irène Hillel-Erlanger killed

---

[25] The pun on the French words "thermomètre" and "thermo-maître" is suggested, but not adequately done justice to, in the English words "thermometer" and "thermo-master". In French, the two words are pronounced identically. (Tr.)

because they feared that the revelations in her book would endanger their activities! Whatever the reason, this fact is not to be neglected: *Voyages en Kaléidoscope* had been dedicated as follows by its author:

> To the Great Soul of L.B., piously, I offer these pages.

Interestingly, in 1919, a certain Louise Barbe, a close friend of the young woman, said to be a chemist – wrongly, for she was above all an alchemist – had died after drinking *potable gold* in excess... doubtlessly overdosed or tampered with! Had she also, in light of the laudatory book dedication by her friend, been the incarnated archetype of Grâce? In any case, she was the first wife of Dr Voronoff, a renowned researcher on the prolongation of life whose research is still republished today. Director of the laboratories of the Collège de France, his experiments in life prolongation involved, among other things, the grafting of monkey testicles. He did more than 500 grafts on animals, and then on humans, in particular, on well-known political, literary personalities, etc.[26]

The poet-hermetist André Savoret understood that the alchemical knowledge of the author of *Voyages en Kaléidoscope* was vast:

> This time I will contribute a modest stone to the edifice of hermetic poetry by evoking an authentic, almost contemporary alchemist whom, I think, I am entitled to call an Adept, and whose writings are practically impossible to find. I mean Irène Hillel-Erlanger...

And going on about her enigmatic book:

> A singular book, the baroque gangue of which hides or protects some ten precious pages constituting evidence traditionally left by any Adept at the moment of his metamorphosis, either by following the fate common to mortals, or – and it is probably the case here – by becoming an avatar of an entirely different order...

Who was being referred to in this remark? In any case, André Savoret is not reluctant in the lines that follow to invite the reader to read the poem that opens the last book written by Irène Hillel-

---

[26] Dr Serge Voronoff, *Etude sur la vieillesse et le rajeunissement par la greffe, Studies on Aging and Youth through Grafting*. (Tr.) éd. Siences en situation, 1999.

Erlanger, entitled *Allégorie liminaire*[27]. Here we will only give the following carefully selected strophe

> Under the **fire of the Sun** [*Emphasis PR*], under the light of Ursa,
> Goes the pilgrim ascending lofty paths,
> But, at last arrived at the end of his course,
> In a secret garden he will find the source,
> The pomegranate and the rose, and the temple of a god.

Irène Hillel-Erlanger was also associated with another female alchemist who became famous in literature; the Russian author, Krisanovskaya, of whom only one book has been translated into French, *L'Élixir de Vie*[28], published by Gallimard in 1927. She was the wife of the prominent scholar Krisanovsky who became Chairman of the Academy of Sciences of the former USSR after the 1917 Revolution, which leads us to believe that mainstream science and alchemy are not necessarily incompatible!

In the year 1926, Éditions Jean Schemit in Paris published an enigmatic alchemical book entitled, *Le Mystère des Cathédrales*[29], signed by one . . . . Fulcanelli.

---

[27] *Liminary Allegory*. (Tr.)

[28] *The Elixir of Life*. (Tr.)

[29] *The Mystery of the Cathedrals*. (Tr.)

FULCANELLI

# LE MYSTÈRE DES CATHÉDRALES

ET L'INTERPRÉTATION ÉSOTÉRIQUE
DES SYMBOLES HERMÉTIQUES
DU GRAND-ŒUVRE

PRÉFACE DE E. CANSELIET, F. C. H.

*Ouvrage illustré de trente-six planches
d'après les dessins de*
JULIEN CHAMPAGNE

PARIS
JEAN SCHEMIT, LIBRAIRE
52, RUE LAFFITTE, 52

1926

*Title page of first edition of* Le Mystère des Cathédrales

# II
# The Alchemical *Mystery of the Cathedrals*

In the heyday of the Roaring Twenties, which enthusiastically acclaimed the arrival of the Charleston from across the Ocean, three hundred copies of a strange book were published to general indifference by publisher Jean Schemit, residing at 52 rue Laffitte. However, this was to subsequently become the much celebrated, *Le Mystère des Cathédrales - The Mystery of the Cathedrals*. The book, signed under the *nom de plume*, Fulcanelli, became a favourite topic of the press and general conversation. In the preface, a young man, aged twenty-six, Eugène Canseliet, announced that the enigmatic author of the book had disappeared well before its publication.

**Fragments from the Preface by Eugène Canseliet**

We read in the preface, dated October 1925:

The author of this book is no longer with us, *and has not been for a long time*.[30] The man faded away, and only his memory remains. I cannot without sorrow recall the image of that industrious and wise Master to whom I owe everything, and lament that he so soon departed. [...]

Thanks to him, the gothic Cathedral confides its secrets. And it is not without surprise or emotion that we learn how our ancestors cut the first stone of the foundations, that dazzling gem, more precious than gold itself, on which Jesus built his church. All truth, all philosophy, and all religion rest upon this unique and sacred stone. Many people,

---

[30] *Emphasis mine.-PR.*

inflated with presumption, believe themselves capable of fashioning it; yet how rare are the elect, those who are unpretentious, learned, and skilful enough to achieve it! But this matters little. It is enough for us to know that the wonders of our Middle Ages contain the same positive truth, the same scientific basis as the pyramids of Egypt, the temples of Greece, the catacombs of Rome, and the Byzantine basilicas.

Such is the overall scope of Fulcanelli's book.

Hermeticists - at least those who are worthy of that name - will discover something else in it....

## The Mystery of the Cathedrals

Let me immediately make it clear to the reader that it is impossible for me, within the narrow frame of this essay, to discuss the real 'hermetic' sense of Fulcanelli's works, so I kindly invite him to refer to my previous books relating to the subject of Alchemy.

The book (whose full title was *Le Mystère des Cathédrales et l'interprétation ésotérique des symboles hermétiques du Grand Oeuvre*[31]*)*, lavishly interspersed with thirty-six illustrations - two of which are in colour, and one that is the original title-page by the artist Jean-Julien Champagne - is curiously dedicated to the *Frères d'Héliopolis*[32]. This refers the reader to the mysteries of the ancient Egyptian religious city evoked on the book's frontispiece, where one observes the Sphinx of Gizeh contemplating a star-laden sky behind the legendary alchemical laboratory. We shall return to this enigmatic dedication submitted to the reader's sagacity later.

### *The Origins of Gothic Art*

Before scrupulously studying – as far as hermetic tradition is concerned - the truly alchemical symbolism emanating from the cathedrals of Notre-Dame de Paris and Notre-Dame d'Amiens, Jacques-Coeur's palace and the Lallemant town-house in Bourges, Fulcanelli offers the reader in his introduction some particularly original concepts that deserve to be emphasized in more than one

---

[31] *The Mystery of the Cathedrals and the Esoteric Interpretation of the Hermetic Symbols of the Great Work.* (Tr.)
[32] The Brothers of Heliopolis. (Tr.)

respect. First, he puzzles over the definition and origins of Gothic Art. He expresses his emotion by reiterating something written by J. F. Colifs in his *Filiation généalogique de toutes les écoles gothiques*[33] (Paris, éditions Baudry, 1884):

> The Language of Stone spoken in this new art, as stated with much truth by J. F. Colifs, is at the same time clear and sublime. This is why it speaks equally to both the soul of the humblest and to that of the most scholarly. What an inspiring and stirring language, the gothic [language] of stones.

After reviewing a few hypotheses about the origins of gothic art, initially those in which the classical school had linked it - against all verisimilitude - to the Goths or Germans, Fulcanelli comes round to linking the word *gothic* to the word *goetic*, via the famous phonetic Cabala referred to previously, thus considering it a magical art. This hypothesis, however, *does not satisfy* him. He then decides to favour the perfect phonetic closeness to the word *argotique*[34], which relates to both slang/cant and to the green language due to its aliveness and vitality, and the Greek myth of the Argonauts who were on a quest for the famous Golden Fleece. The "Argotiers" could only be the symbolic descendants who expressed themselves in a vivid language not understood by the uninitiated. He writes on this point:

> People still say about a very intelligent, but rather cunning man: *he knows everything, he understands argot (slang)*. All initiates expressed themselves in argot: the vagrants of the Court of Miracles (*Cour des Miracles*) - headed by the poet Villon - as well as the Freemasons of the Middle Ages, 'members of the lodge of God', who built the argothic masterpieces we admire today. Those 'builder-sailors' (nautes) also knew the route to the Garden of the Hesperides.

According to Fulcanelli, the minority of individuals using this secret (and sacred) language constitute the *Sons or Children of the Sun*, the gothic art being indeed the "art *got* or *cot* (*Xo*), the art of *Light* or of the Spirit". And Fulcanelli elaborates on this universal language of the birds, the diplomatic language taught by the goddess Athena to the seer Tiresias.

---

[33] *Genealogical Filiation of all Gothic Schools.* (Tr.)
[34] Slang. (Tr.)

From the start of *The Mystery of the Cathedrals*, the tune is set: the teachings delivered by the Master will be most original, because the phonetic Cabala will give the key. His friend, the archaeologist Grasset d'Orcet[35], had already revealed the rules of it in his writings.

## Interpretation of the Imagery

The singular research by G. J. Witkowski in *L'Art profane à l'Eglise*[36] led him to conjure up the most disconcerting scenes, often tinged with eroticism and unusual elements present in gothic cathedrals, but which served Fulcanelli in that he was able to extract from them the hermetic "substantive marrow". Let us mention that another book by the same author, also published by Jean Schemit - the future publisher of Fulcanelli, let us not forget - was entitled *L'Art chrétien, ses Licences symboliques, satiriques, fantaisistes*[37].

The Master quotes an eloquent excerpt from the first of these two books about the nave in Notre-Dame de Strasbourg:

> The bas-relief on one of the capitals of the great pillars represents a satirical procession, in which a piglet may be seen bearing a holy stoup, followed by donkeys wearing priestly garments, and monkeys bearing various religious attributes, as well as a fox enclosed in a shrine. It is the *Procession of the Fox*, or the *Feast of the Donkey*.

Similarly, Fulcanelli states that the Feast of Fools - or of the Wise, when one thinks of the symbolism in the $22^{nd}$ Tarot arcanum - was celebrated in the Middle Ages as a hermetic processional kermis (festival) and used to set out from the cathedral with its pope, its clergy and the crowd of believers, and then move through the city. The Triumphal Chariot of Bacchus would then move off, drawn by a male and female centaur. It was accompanied by the god Pan, goddesses Juno, Diana, Venus, and Leto, and an entourage of nymphs and naïads, all running around sparsely clad in an unbridled, enthusiastic and festive carnival atmosphere. They would all converge on the cathedral, and Fulcanelli reveals that it is the

---

[35] Grasset d'Orcet "Matériaux cryptographiques" in *Revue britannique*, republished by B. Allieu and A. Barthélémy, Paris, 1979.
[36] *The Secular Art of the Church.* (Tr.) éditions Schemit, 1908
[37] *Christian Art, its Symbolic, Satirical and Fanciful Liberties.* (Tr.)

archbishop of Sens, Pierre de Corbeil - himself a hermetic initiate - who composed this mass, which although seemingly a parody, was imbued with undisputed alchemical symbolism. The Master adds:

> Finally, there were some bizarre events in which a hermetic meaning, often a very precise one, is discernible. These were held every year, with the Gothic church as their theatre. Examples include the *Flagellation of the Alleluia*, in which choirboys energetically whipped their humming-tops (*sabots*) [a top with the outline of a *Tau* or *Cross*.] down the aisles of the cathedral of Langres; the *Procession of the Shrovetide Carnival*; the *Devilry of Chaumont*; the procession and banquets of the Dijon infantry (*Infanterie dijonnaise*). The latter was the last echo of the *Feast of Fools*, with its *Mad Mother*, its bawdy diplomas, its banner on which two brothers, lying head to foot, delighted in uncovering their buttocks. Until 1538, when the custom died out, a strange *Ball Game* (Pelota) was played inside Saint Etienne, the cathedral of Auxerre.

Victor Hugo masterfully recreated this atmosphere in his *Notre-Dame de Paris*, largely inspired by an anonymous hermeticist using the pseudonym of Magistri who pretended he was able to make gold. The Quasimodo character plays the part of the fool during the eponymous celebration, but also represents the raw stone that allows us to achieve the Great Work. All of which makes this masterpiece a true synopsis of alchemical science.

Victor Hugo, who saw in Notre-Dame de Paris the most gratifying epitomes of hermetic science, also wrote:

> In the Middle Ages, humankind never obtained any significant knowledge that they did not write in stone.

According to the Tradition, alchemists met every Saturday in the courtyard of Notre-Dame de Paris to discuss the Great Work. One of them, Denys Zachaire, tells us that this custom was still alive in 1539, but then only on Sundays and holidays. Fulcanelli states in passing that during the Middle Ages this cathedral was adorned with various colours: "*There, amid a dazzling array of painted and gilded arches, of string-courses and copings, of tympana with multi-coloured figures, each philosopher would show the result of his labours and work out the next sequence of his researches.*" Fulcanelli also reveals that Guillaume de Paris, who was responsible for the bas-reliefs of the western façade, had also taken great care to meticulously reproduce the motifs of the medallions on the stained glass panes of the central rose-window.

*Alchemical Symbolism*

Deploring what he called, "Soufflot's vandalism", Fulcanelli extends his gratitude to the renovation work in Notre-Dame undertaken by the distinguished architects Viollet-le-Duc, Lassus, and Geoffroy Dechaume. He then examines the ground plan of medieval religious buildings where he sees the image of the Egyptian ankh (*crux ansata* - that is, the *ansated,* or *"handled"* or *"looped" cross*) in the semi-circular apse joined to the choir. This is the symbolic evocation, not of death, but of universal Life upon which is built the Christian temple. In addition, he states - by way of the phonetic Cabala - that the cross (*crux*) designates the alchemist's *crucible.*

Following this, Fulcanelli discusses the enigmatic labyrinths that are found in some churches such as those in Sens, Reims, Auxerre, Saint-Quentin, Poitiers, Bayeux, Chartres, and, above all, Amiens, to which he devotes an entire chapter later on in the book. Reminding us of the labyrinth's presence in ancient times, mentioning, among others, the one in Cnossos, (Crete)[38]. He calls the labyrinth of the cathedrals *"Solomon's Labyrinth"* and gives the definition of it expressed by his prominent friend Marcellin Berthelot:

> [It is] a cabbalistic figure found at the beginning of certain alchemical manuscripts, and which is part of the magical tradition associated with the name of Solomon. It is a series of concentric circles, interrupted at certain points, so as to form a bizarre and inextricable path.

Fulcanelli then embarks on a philosophical digression (in the alchemical sense of the term) on the myth of Ariadne and her legendary thread.

Next, Fulcanelli brings our attention to the alchemical symbolism to be found in the rose-windows of the cathedrals. He compares their

---

[38] Cf. Patrick Rivière, *Histoire comparative des religions et des mythes*, éditions Ramuel, 1999.

blazing colours to the ones developed in the *Egg* during the coction of the third Work[39] under the impulse of the *fire of the wheel*, an expression meant to designate the action of the "secret fire" in the ultimate phase of the Great Work. He states that it is "*this latter fire, sustained by ordinary heat, which makes the wheel turn and produces the various phenomena which the artist observes in his vessel*".

After this, Fulcanelli deals with the question of the "black Virgins" (*virgini pariturae - the virgin about to give birth*) in Chartres, Rocamadour, Puy-en-Velay, Limoux, and the unusual green-candle ceremony at Saint Victor church in Marseilles. Comparing the black Virgin to the ancient mother goddesses, Ceres, Rhea, and Isis, he identifies her with the symbolism in which is clad the mysterious *materia prima* of the Great Work.

Fulcanelli then proceeds with a long critique of the Renaissance period, favouring the spirit that characterised the medieval mind:

> The builders of the Middle Ages had the natural attributes of faith and modesty. The anonymous creators of pure works of art, they built for Truth, for the affirmation of their ideal, for the propagation and the nobility of their science. Those of the Renaissance, preoccupied above all by their personality, jealous of their worth, built for their own future fame.

Further on Fulcanelli studies certain medallions on the central porch of the western façade of Notre-Dame de Paris and gives these a truly alchemical interpretation, far removed from the studies previously carried out by the hermeticists Cambriel and Gobineau de Montluisant. The portal on the right, where can be admired the image of Saint Marcellus defeating a dragon and freeing a child held in limbo, perfectly illustrates to Fulcanelli the major operations in the alchemical Great Work.

Fulcanelli then takes us to the Cathedral of Notre-Dame de Amiens and finds in its central porch - the Porch of the Saviour - the same symbols as in Notre-Dame de Paris, the only difference being that here the figures are holding shields rather than discs, and that

---

[39] Cf. Patrick Rivière, *Alchimie: science et mystique*, éditions De Vecchi.

the philosopher's mercury is represented as a woman, and not as a man as in Paris. He then discusses the *fire of the wheel* and the scale of temperatures in the Great Work.

Continuing, Fulcanelli takes his readers to Bourges where the Lallemant mansion and the great house of Jacques Coeur hold his attention. King Charles VII's great Minister of Finances[40] was indeed an alchemist, and hermetic symbols are plentiful in his noble abode. However, such symbols can be seen in perhaps greater abundance in Jean Lallemant's residence, particularly on the enigmatic coffered ceiling, in the chapel, and its credence, which holds the secrets of the second and third Work.

Interestingly, the last chapter, which was dedicated to the cyclic cross of Hendaye, was not included in the first edition of *The Mystery of the Cathedrals*. This is a matter we shall discuss later on.

---

[40] i.e. Jacques Coeur (Tr.).

# III
## Dwellings of the Philosophers

Fulcanelli's second book, *Dwellings of the Philosophers*[41], was originally one volume consisting of some six hundred pages divided into twenty chapters. In his foreword of the book, written in April 1929, Eugène Canseliet reveals the key enabling one to penetrate his master's writings. It lies in the following excerpt:

> His method differs from the one that was used by his predecessors: it consists in describing in detail all the operations of the Work after having separated them into various parts. He thus deals with each phase of the work, begins to explain it in one chapter, interrupts it to pursue it in another chapter, and then completes it in yet a last one. This breaking up, which transforms the Magisterium into a philosophical jig-saw puzzle, is not to scare the learned researcher, but it promptly discourages the outsider, incapable of finding his way in this labyrinth of another kind, and unable to restore the order of the manipulations.

(Let me again make clear that in this particular work, I can in no way pierce the hidden meaning of the allegories of alchemical operations. To this end, I strongly recommend to the reader my previous books devoted to alchemy (op. cit.).)

### Volume One

At the beginning of the book, Fulcanelli reverts to the subject of stone edifices; the custodians of hermetic science:

---

[41] *Les Demeures philosophales.* (Tr.)

> [...] Our preference remains for the Middle Ages such as revealed by the gothic edifices, rather than that period of time as described by historians.

Further on, he alludes to Huysmans' statement:

> History is the most solemn of lies and the most childish of catches!

He seizes that opportunity to question the authenticity of certain tombs - crypts allegedly containing the remains of this or that historical figure, maintaining that it stands to reason that they are empty, unless corpses were substituted! He then again evokes the primacy of the Middle Ages over the period of the Renaissance:

> [...] We deem that the medieval way of thinking reveals itself as being of scientific essence and no other. Art and literature are merely humble servants of traditional science. Their specific mission is to translate into symbols the truths that the Middle Ages received from Antiquity and of which they remained the faithful repositories.

In the next chapter, Fulcanelli gives some definitions of the term *alchemy*[42] and pays tribute to the Adepts of the past. He then evokes the image of the legendary laboratory with its picturesque character.

In the following chapter, entitled *"Chimie et Philosophie"*, Fulcanelli makes a distinction between alchemy and mere chemistry. He describes the first as the "science of causes" and the second as "science of facts". In his opinion, the latter rests on matter and experimentation, while the first originates in philosophy:

> Thus, contrary to philosophy, which anticipates facts, and assures the orientation of ideas and their practical connections, theory, conceived afterwards, modified according to the results of experiment as they were acquired, always reflects the uncertainty of temporary things and gives to modern science the character of a perpetual empiricism. A large quantity of chemical facts, seriously observed, are impervious to logics and are beyond all reasoning.

---

[42] Cf. *Alchimie: science et mystique*, éditions De Vecchi.

*Title page of the first edition of* Les Demeures philosophales

Fulcanelli quotes a certain number of cases that resist a purely chemical analysis; for instance, gold, which ordinarily requires only *aqua regia* as a solvent. How can it dissolve so easily in a cold solution of potassium cyanide? Similarly, why does sulphur chloride, composed of two elements, each of which combines in incandescence with potassium, have no action whatsoever on this metal?

Fulcanelli then touches upon the subject of the potential fire enclosed in matter and defines alchemy as securing the bond that unites God to Nature, Creation to its Creator, and true science to revealed religion. He then makes mention of numerous scientific treatises and deplores that an open mind, which should be the very nature of scientists, is indeed such a rare quality in them, leaving us with the understanding that he belongs to this circle with which he is so well acquainted.

In the next chapter Fulcanelli makes a point of explaining the hermetic Cabala, which is based on phonetic assonance as well as on certain rules resting on the study of ancient Greek - the language of the Hellenes, and before them of the Pelasgians - perhaps of the very gods themselves! It is the language of the birds, the *gay science* or *gay sçavoir*, which enables the initiate to express Knowledge in only veiled terms[43].

One recognizes in this treatise, admirable in more ways than one, the author's *deep knowledge of chemistry*. Illustrating this in the next chapter, entitled *"Alchimie et spagyrie"*, Fulcanelli emphasizes the differences between noble Alchemy (where the tapping of cosmic energy - *Spiritus Mundi* - is all-important, since spirit drives matter) and the somewhat empirical processes that in some cases enabled unauthentic alchemists - the so-called "puffers" - to achieve "aurific tinctures" with some success, mainly to coin counterfeit money!

Here Fulcanelli describes very precisely the *modus operandi* that allows one to achieve the so-called "aurific tinctures" that he names "trivial matters", showing us even more clearly than before that there can be no doubt about his thorough scientific schooling. The result of this is quite astounding. So great is his mastery of mineral

---

[43] Cf. The numerous examples supplied in our book: *Alchimie: science et mystique*.

chemistry and his ingeniousness in this domain that, to our knowledge, *none of the processes described by him had ever been referred to before by any of his predecessors* - not by Jollivet-Castelot's team, nor Dr Joubert, nor even by the works of Greek authors made public by Marcellin Berthelot. Moreover, he discloses the secret of one of the processes of which the good Saint Vincent de Paul, charity's apostle, had been acquainted, thanks to an old man who had given him a home in Tunis and had saved him from slavery in 1605. This indeed deeply interested the Vice-Legate in Avignon, and the good abbot then had no difficulty in obtaining his introduction to Rome, the Eternal City.

**Second Volume**

After this, Fulcanelli undertakes the actual study of certain historic buildings that are adorned with alchemical symbols, and which he names "the dwellings of the philosophers". The *Manoir de la Salamandre*[44] in Lisieux (no longer in existence) is the first one he deals with. Fulcanelli suggests that within its walls there existed a fraternity of Adepts - the Flers Alchemists, in the Orne Department - that counted the following three men among its members in 1420: Nicolas de Grosparmy, Nicolas Valois, and the priest, Pierre Vicot. This small group alone is said to have moved to Caen (Calvados Department), and one of the members allegedly erected the *Manoir de la Salamandre* in the course of the following century. Fulcanelli discusses at length the *Secret Fire* of the Great Work in this chapter. This *Secret Fire* is allegorically represented by a salamander, and according to legend, it lives in the igneous element. Several pages farther along, Fulcanelli lists the multiple virtues of the philosopher's stone. Drawing on various texts by the scholarly librarian, Pierre Dujols, he also brings our attention to the alchemical symbolism emanating from the Graal[45] and the Templars' *Baphomet*[46].

---

[44] The Manor of the Salamander. (Tr.)

[45] Cf. Patrick Rivière, *Les Secrets du Graal*, éditions De Vecchi, et Le Graal : Histoire et Symboles, éditions du Rocher.

[46] Cf. Patrick Rivière, *Les Templiers et leurs Mystères*, éditions De Vecchi.

Referring to the "house of Adam and Eve" in Le Mans, Fulcanelli also discusses in some detail Genesis and the symbolic appearance of the *first Adam* (made of red earth), and of the *second Adam* (Sulphur) that united with Eve and which designates Mercury.

He then talks about the "reincrudation" of the metal that perishes during the second Work.

In the chapter dedicated to Louis d'Estissac, and recalling the hermetic concerns[47] of the author of *Gargantua* and of *Pantagruel*, Fulcanelli sees in the scholarly François Rabelais the *maître dès alchimies*[48] who initiated young Estissac. In this chapter, Fulcanelli particularly develops his thoughts on the symbolic significance of the Greek letter X (*khi*), since it is this letter that is identified with Light itself. In this respect, he tells us "the Greek X and the French X represent the writing of the light by the light itself". Bringing up Saint-Andrew's cross, as well as cat whiskers in the shape of a cross, he also tells us about the ways and customs of the *Ecole Polytechnique* (the "X"[49]), which *he knows too well* to have not been personally familiar with them! Furthermore, he adds:

> The X is the emblem of measure (metron) taken in all its meanings: dimensions, range, space, duration, rule, law, milestone, or limit. That is the occult reason why the international prototype of the meter, built in iridescent platinum and kept in the Breteuil Pavilion in Sèvres, assumes the profile of an X in its cross-section.

And he adds:

> All bodies obeying this fundamental law of effulgence...are submitted to this measure.

Fulcanelli then tells us about the famous Parisian *Cabaret du Chat-Noir*[50], with which he was also well acquainted, having been a frequent caller there:

---

[47] Cf. Patrick Rivière, *Le Graal : Histoire et Symboles*.

[48] Master of alchemy. (Tr.)

[49] The Ecole polytechnique is the elite school for engineers in France. It is known as "X". (Tr.)

[50] The Black-Cat Club (Tr.).

[...] Many among us remember the celebrated Chat-Noir, which was so popular while under the management of Rodolphe Salis; but how many knew of the esoteric and political centre that was concealed there, of the international masonry that was hidden behind the signboard of the artistic cabaret? On the one hand, the talent of fervent, idealistic youth made up of carefree, blind aesthetes in search of glory and incapable of suspicion; on the other hand, the confidence of a mysterious science mixed with obscure diplomacy - a dual-faced picture deliberately exhibited in a medieval frame. The enigmatic "tournée des grands-ducs"[51], under the sign of the wide-eyed cat in his nocturnal livery, with rigid and over-sized X-shaped whiskers - whose heraldic posture gave to the wings of the Montmartre windmill a symbolic value equal to its own - was not that of princes on the spree.

In the following chapter, entitled *'L'homme des bois'*[52], Fulcanelli refers to the hermetic pilgrimage to Saint James of Compostela, as well as to the Parisian alchemist, Nicolas Flamel.

Fulcanelli then extensively examines the coffered paintings on the ceiling admirably adorning the high gallery in the Château of Dampierre-sur-Boutonn. It should be said that they summarize the full complexity of the achievements of the Second Work's "sublimations".

The prestigious tomb of François II in Nantes provides him with ample material to discourse on the alchemical androgynous state, and thus discuss what sets the hermetic Cabala in opposition to the mysteries of the Hebraïc Kabbala.

In the study of the Holyrood Palace sundial in Edinburgh, Scotland, Fulcanelli gives the reader precious information about the making of the Adepts' famous *vitryol*. Furthermore, he supplies significant details about the hermetic character of the prestigious *Order of the Thistle*, with which Scottish alchemist Alexander Sethon[53] was likely not unfamiliar.

---

[51] A 'turn-of-XXth century' expression born when the emigrated Russian nobility went on 'joy rides' and visited all the 'in' and elegant night clubs of Western Europe, and France in particular. (Tr.)
[52] The Trapper (Tr.).
[53] Alexander Sethon, called "the Cosmopolitan" had the wisdom to conceal his activites all his life until he married. In order to please his wife, who was young and

In its subsequent edition, *The Dwellings of the Philosophers* ends with a chapter entitled "The Unlimited Paradox of Sciences", which is decidedly hermetic in orientation, although also apocalyptic. According to Eugène Canseliet, this section was added to the previous text and was composed of the material of a third "collection of handwritten notes" that his master, Fulcanelli, had left with him before taking them back in 1928, thereby making it impossible to eventually publish the third book. That book, had it been published, would have been entitled *Finis Gloriae Mundi - The End of the Glory of the World*. We will see further on what should be kept in mind on this subject. For the time being, suffice it to say that Eugène Canseliet stated with regard to this book: "Undoubtedly, it was about very serious matters"![54]

**Did Fulcanelli have a master?**

As far as the Work's Gordian knot is concerned, Eugène Canseliet wrote about his master:

> Following the example of Basile Valentin, his true initiator, he was unsuccessful for more than thirty years, unable to find a solution![55]

Does this mean that the works of the Erfurt Benedictine monk referred to in his books were, in his eyes, the only valid teachings that could lead him to success? Having been strongly influenced by his works myself, I can only peremptorily conclude affirmatively.

In his introduction to a new reprint of *Douze Clefs de la Philosophie*[56] by Basile Valentin, Eugène Canseliet again made it clear that:

---

beautiful, he yielded to the invitation extended him by the Elector of Saxony, Christian II, to come to his court. Since Sethon was unwilling to disclose the secret of the Philosopher's Stone, which he had long possessed, he was scalded every day with molten lead, beaten with rods and punctured with needles till he died. (Tr.)

[54] In *Le Feu du Soleil. Entretien sur l'Alchimie* avec Eugène Canseliet, par Robert Amadou, éditions J.-J. Pauvert, Paris, 1978.

[55] First preface to *The Dwellings of the Philosophers*.

[56] *Twelve Keys of Philosophy*, éditions de Minuit, 1980.

After all of these years, we still vividly remember the veneration our old Master Fulcanelli held for Basile Valentin, whom he considered to be his first initiator.

But the disciple thought it advisable to add a *second master* - this time contemporaneous with the anonymous Adept - and therefore included the following for the benefit of the reader of *The Mystery of the Cathedrals* (second preface, 1957):

> In our introduction to *Douze Clefs de la Philosophie*, we deliberately added that Basile Valentin was our Master's *initiator*, partly because this gave us the opportunity to change the epithet of the word, i.e. to substitute - for the sake of accuracy - *first* initiator for *true* initiator, which we had used in our preface to *Les Demeures philosophales*. At that time, we were unaware of the deeply moving letter, which we shall quote a little later, and which owes its amazing beauty to the warm enthusiasm and fervent expression of the writer. Both the writer and recipient remain anonymous, because the signature has been scratched out and there is no superscription. The recipient was undoubtedly Fulcanelli's master, and Fulcanelli left this revealing letter among his own papers. It bears two crossed brown lines at the folds, from having been kept for so long in his pocketbook, which did not, however, protect it from the fine, greasy dust of the enormous stove going all the time. So, for many years, the author of *Le Mystère des Cathédrales* kept the written proof of the triumph of his *true initiator* as a talisman.*[...]*

But the question still remains to be asked, i.e. what indeed was his true identity in the civil status books?

# IV
# The Legendary Encounter between Fulcanelli and Eugène Canseliet

Eugène Canseliet, who became Fulcanelli's disciple and eventually devoted his entire life to Alchemy, was born to an honourable though modest family on December 18, 1899 in Sarcelles, a region of Paris. His father was a skilled sculptor-mason, and the young Canseliet inherited undeniable artistic talents; talents which manifested throughout his life via not only his literary work, but also by way of his drawings and water-colours. A gifted sketcher, his parents decided to allow him to pursue his studies further upon completion of a brilliant classical secondary education. Thus, in 1913, they took him to an entrance examination organized by the *Atelier d'Art Parisien Andrès et Brenner*[57], located at 43 rue de l'Echiquier. Eugène Canseliet described the event that was going to have such a significant influence on his destiny in an interview with Robert Amadou:

> The examination was scheduled to last for one hour. When the hour had elapsed, the exam inspector said (I can still see and hear that bearded man): "Children, it is over." Some of the children bustled up from their places. They were already through. "I have seen your efforts," stated the inspector. "There is one sketcher among you; only one. It is him," he said, pointing at me. "But Sir, I have not yet finished." "It is good," he responded. "It is enough for me."[58]

---

[57] Parisian art school. (Tr.)
[58] *Le Feu du Soleil*, J. J. Pauvert, 1978.

From that day forward, the young Canseliet knew that he was going to devote himself to his art, while simultaneously following classical studies. Strongly attracted to mysticism, he spent his free time reading the works of Papus, Stanislas de Guaïta and Edouard Schuré - the author of *Les Grands Initiés*[59].

One night, disturbed by a strange dream, he abruptly awoke and jotted down an enigmatic message in Latin, the translation of which is as follows:

> When black ravens have begotten white doves in your house, you will be then called The Wise.

In 1915, he discovered a reprint of *Hermès Dévoilé*[60], the alchemical opuscule signed by Cyliani that we have previously mentioned, and the young man fell for the romantic charm of that singular work. He then felt arise within him - as he himself described it - an intense desire to follow the alchemical quest. His enthusiasm for this chosen path would never subside, as his history testifies.

**The Legendary Encounter**

While studying Fine Arts in Marseilles in 1915, he occasionally opened up a little bit to the old lady who did the cleaning in the workshops - herself an adept of zouave Jacob, as it happened. One day she told him:

> I would like to introduce you to a gentleman who owns some very old books. You'll see. He'll certainly like you. I do the cleaning at his place.

And there, barely 400 yards from Place Carli where the Fine Arts buildings were located, at 4 rue Dieudé, was a beautiful building that was the home of the local library. It also accommodated a bookbinder[61] by the name of **Ch. Violette**[62], who received the young man with kindness. In fact, this was the very same man who would

---

[59] *The Grand Initiates*. (Tr.)

[60] *Hermes Unmasked*. (Tr.)

[61] It is easy to trace him in the Marseilles' street directory: year 1915, p. 1154.

[62] CH.V., = C.H.F. or F.C.H.: the initials associated with the name of Fulcanelli in the titles of his writings, and in those of Eugène Canseliet, his disciple.

become famous some years later under the pseudonym of *Fulcanelli*. And this is the reason why Eugène Canseliet so often alluded to '*violets*' in his writings. But was *Violette* Fulcanelli's real patronym, or was it an alias? That is the question.

Thus, while WWI was raging on the European front, the meeting between the two men had taken place most simply. Eugène Canseliet had found his master who, after a trial period of a few months, initiated him into the reading of the old alchemical texts.

"Discussions went on," stated Eugène Canseliet[63], "to which, under the light of a huge petroleum lamp, the crowd of authors assembled in the adjoining library were often invited as witnesses."

Already at that time, Fulcanelli clearly invited his young disciple to master the art of writing with:

Write as you draw!

This was in 1916, and that year the young disciple met an individual at the Master's residence who had already been in his service for a number of years. This was the painter, Jean-Julien Champagne, who became friends with the young Canseliet, despite the fact that he was twenty-two years the young man's senior. Champagne had been a pupil of Léon Gérôme at the Paris Fine Arts School. His talents as a water-colourist were undeniable, which undoubtedly contributed in bringing these two men closer together.

The following year, Canseliet left Marseilles for Aix-en-Provence in order to successfully obtain his diploma in classical humanities. During this time, according to Canseliet,

Fulcanelli frequently came to visit. On one of these visits, at La Fouranne, Fulcanelli supposedly told him:

In the very first place, know and love, deeply, the language of France, *propter hanc causam quod principii verbum absolutissima est.*

Later on, at Lycée Charlemagne in the region of Paris, Canseliet completed his Latin studies. At practically the same time, Fulcanelli also went back to Paris.

---

[63] In *Les Demeures philosophales*, second preface by Eugène Canseliet.

Jean-Julien Champagne, like Fulcanelli, also paid Eugène Canseliet visits, and their friendship grew ever stronger. Champagne was often a guest of the illustrious de Lesseps family that counted among its members Ferdinand (deceased in 1894), widely renown for the construction of the Suez Canal, and his descendants, Bertrand and Paul-Bertrand, for whom Champagne sometimes did work.

One autumn day in 1919, when Jean-Julien Champagne and Eugène Canseliet were standing at the entrance to the Lesseps' town-house on avenue Montaigne, they noticed Fulcanelli having a discussion in the yard with the former Prime Minister, René Viviani, whose carriage was waiting in the avenue. After the Master had taken leave of Viviani, he noticed that Eugène Canseliet was wearing a mourning band around his left arm. He questioned the young man about this, who told him that it was for his grandmother who had died a few months before and to whom he had been very much attached. He added that she had been eighty when she died, to which Fulcanelli replied:

"Why! Exactly my age!"

Which, of course, would have meant that he had been born around 1840.

It would seem that at that time, Fulcanelli was residing in Paris not far from the building of the Beaux Arts school, near the gardens and close to the Temple de l'Amitié, on rue Jacob. The adjoining street, Saint-Benoît, does indeed suggest Fulcanelli's actual master, the Benedictine monk-alchemist, Basile Valentin.

His house consisted of a basement, a raised ground floor, and a second floor. The eight large rooms in the house were lighted by twelve windows. There was a narrow terrace at the top of the staircase, which was enclosed by a light balustrade, while the mysterious laboratory was located in the basement. It is there that Fulcanelli laboured on the Great Work with the purpose of achieving the Philosopher's stone.

*Ferdinand de Lesseps*

We can allow ourselves to inquire into the importance of the reconstruction of facts made possible from the statements of Eugène Canseliet, which were collected throughout his life.

What if the initial meeting had taken place in Paris rather than in Marseilles? Indeed, when one is familiar with the hermeticists' immoderate taste for their *solar cabala*, it is permitted for us to imagine arriving at the centre of the capital city, not far from *Arts et Métiers*[64], to find *rue d'Aix*; or better yet, the *rue Dieu*[65] and parallel to it *rue de Marseille*, a diagonal line joining them up to *quai de Valmy* (which goes up to *cité Jacob*) as (by lucky chance!) the *rue . . . Beaurepaire*[66] (the one belonging to the Master, of course), as if being pointed at by *God's own finger*!

As to Fulcanelli's last home, close to the *Temple de l'Amitié*[67] on *rue Jacob*, let us wager that one could have discovered it - in view of the frequent alluding to the love the latter had for cats (see further

---

[64] The Arts and Trade school in Paris. (Tr.)
[65] God street (Tr.).
[66] Beautiful Den (Tr.).
[67] Temple of Friendship (Tr.).

on) - in *rue de l'Echaudé*[68] (referring to the well known proverb: a scalded cat fears cold water)!

And here we are consumed with the desire to get closer to the true personality of the Adept temporarily identified as a certain bookbinder by the nickname of *Violette*. We shall see what conclusions we come to, particularly in light of the fact that Eugène Canseliet frequently alluded to this name, either by numerous references to Viollet-le-Duc, who, in passing, might have been one of Fulcanelli's friends, or by the recurring reference to a Renaissance alchemist, one Joseph Duchêne, who was better known under the pseudonym of our Mr de Violette, esq.

**Close to the Athanor**

Young Eugène Canseliet met his master quite often. He was, one might say, in his proximity, though not in his intimacy. Long philosophical digressions, washed down with the cold, sugared coffee Fulcanelli was so fond of, were interspersed with numerous observations of the Matter evolving within the Athenor. The studious disciple later remembered these fantastic evenings as:

A privilege we enjoyed (*he is speaking of himself*), finding oneself for such a long time near the Master, as a witness filled with wonder of his indefatigable manipulations at the fire-hole of the furnace[69].

And then Fulcanelli turned the discussion again to the original Matter of the Great Work:

"They (*the hermetic philosophers*) rightly considered it to be a very real gift from the Creator, and they firmly stated that without divine inspiration, one would never be able, in this outcast magma, repellent in its aspect, to recognize the gift from God that transforms the simple alchemist into a Sage and the philosopher into a proven Adept.... See Eyrenee Philalethes, who assimilates it with gold and gives it its name. Look at Chapter XVIII, paragraph III, of his *Introitus*," concluded Fulcanelli, drawing on his prodigious memory with all the benevolence of his good smile, and with one hand risen

---

[68] Scalded Street. (Tr.)

[69] Cf. Patrick Rivière, *Les Templiers et leurs Mystères*, éditons De Vecchi.

in a customary gesture, on which was shining that evening the baphometic ring carved in transmutated gold that had come to him from the Templars of the Hennebont Commandery in Brittany.

From where did that mysterious ring come? That ring formed from transmutated gold upon which was carved the Templars' Baphomet[70] and which was adorned with alchemical symbols? Obviously, from the scholarly librarian, Pierre Dujols, aka Magophon (cf. Chapter One), whose wife was a native of Hennebont in Brittany. In fact, that fabulous ring came from the abbot of the Cistercian monastery that existed near the Templar Commandery in the 12$^{th}$ century. It is said that Fulcanelli had known Pierre Dujols for a number of years and that both men had become close friends due to their common interest in hermetic matters. This is unequivocally evidenced by the dedication adorning the *Hypotypose* Dujols wrote as commentary to the *Mutus Liber*, given to Fulcanelli by the learned librarian. It states as follows:

## *Mutus Liber*

*To my old and good friend*
*To the Adept-Philosopher,*
Ingeniosis apertum,
Stolidisque sigillatum,
Hunc offero tibi lectum
Pro nobis enucleatum

Magophon – Pierre Dujols,
18 March 1920[71]

The Latin text reads: "Open to the ingenious and sealed to the fools, I am offering you this reading for us who are enlightened."

This illustrates the degree of familiarity between Pierre Dujols and Fulcanelli! It is true that Fulcanelli was particularly fond of the hermetic librarian, the more so as the latter descended in direct line

---

[70] On 18 March, and curiously, on the day of the commemoration of the martyrdom of the Order of the Temple's last master (18 March 1314). Cf. our book *Les Templiers et leurs Mystères*.

[71] In *Légende liminaire des deux Logis alchimiques*, Eugène Canseliet, éditions J.-J. Pauvert, Paris.

from the last Valois-Angoulême, as we have already mentioned. Furthermore, Fulcanelli was of the habit of rubbing elbows with famous politicians such as René Viviani, Jules Grévy - the late President of the Third Republic - as well as Paul Painlevé, a former Prime Minister. He was also well acquainted with many scientists and artists who frequented the de Lesseps town-house, such as writer Raymond Roussel, whom Eugène Canseliet referred to in the following terms for the benefit of the leading man of the Surrealist movement, André Breton:

> [...] amongst the various people whom we saw around the Master at avenue Montaigne - always highly qualified or renown - Raymond Roussel impressed us the most. Consequently, it appeared to us quite odd that our old friend, Julien Champagne, would call that distinguished man "la classe"[72]. It is true that both men had belonged to the same contingent - the one of 1877 - and that Mr Roussel, who had a passion for the internal combustion engine, admired Fulcanelli's and Bertrand de Lesseps's draftsman. It is also true that Champagne was the inventor of the screw-propeller sleigh created for Ferdinand's eldest son and which was admired by Raymond Roussel at avenue Montaigne[73]....

Fulcanelli's last dwelling was spacious. Past the entrance, one could see into the study where a solid mahogany cupboard in which his oldest and most valuable books were kept. Among those was a seventeenth-century manuscript copy of *De la Nature à découvert, pour les Enfants de la Science seulement et non pour les Ignorants Sophistes*[74], by the Unknown Knight (cf. *Trois anciens Traités d'Alchimie*[75], editions J. J. Pauvert, Paris). At that time, it was still possible to catch a glimpse of the trees in the nearby garden through the three large windows in this room that boasted of parquetry inlaid with Hungarian motifs. Later on, Eugène Canseliet wrote in his *Alchimiques Mémoires* that:

---

[72] The annual contingent of recruits. (Tr.)

[73] We shall revert later to Jean-Julien Champagne's overall ingeniousness, and to his talents as an inventor in particular.

[74] *Nature Uncovered, For the Children of the Science Only, and not for Ignorant Sophists.* (Tr.)

[75] *Three Ancient Treatises on Alchemy.* (Tr.)

Under the attic, there was a small door leading to the terrace above the staircase, which was enclosed by an exquisite balustrade of white stone. Up there, one walked on a thick carpet of lead. This was the most elevated place in the open air, where the Master submitted to the radiation of the Moon and of the stars, his basins containing a dew that was already very gently reduced. In my mind, I can still see those white porcelain containers, rectangular, shallow, 18 x 24 cm, the original use of which was for developing photographs. [...] On the discrete terrace of which I just evoked the moving memory, a robin, full of elegant boldness, was frequently seen hopping about under the watchful gaze of Fulcanelli, who called it 'my little rubiette'. It had practically become a pet, and to my amazement, Fulcanelli took very great pleasure in talking to it in the language of the birds [...]. The Master told me that his cats had taught him this idiom, which remains the exclusive right of the birds' world!

In the year 1920, Fulcanelli similarly remarked to his disciple, as recorded in his diary:

My young friend, you will find alchemy in every noble domain; within what is most humble, as within what is most high. You will need to seek it tirelessly in order to reach the triumphal conclusion.

In that same year, 1920, Eugène Canseliet became an employee in the accounting department of the Sarcelles gasworks. The Georgi Company gave him a small room upstairs into which he moved, and there he installed a modest laboratory where he could carry out all sorts of alchemical operations. It was there that he achieved - on the Master's recommendations, obviously - the resolution of a more *archemical* than *alchemical* process, a process envisaged by the ancient author of the *Traité du Feu et du Sel*[76], Blaise de Vigenère, and based on the fusion of common lead. He carried out this *"little particular"* and ended up with a real success that exulted and thrilled Fulcanelli.

Prior to carrying out the experiment (*wrote the young disciple*), it is impossible to conceive of the deep changes in the composition of apparently simple bodies that are brought about by slow processing and prolonged fusion. Although their inner structure and outer aspects seem to be little affected, one realises quite quickly in the

---

[76] *Treatise on Fire and Salt.* (Tr.)

subsequent operations how thoroughly they are actually modified chemically. It is a quite simple method - although in compliance with both the example given by Nature, and the rules of the Great Art - and which makes the extraction of Saturn's specific mercury particularly easy ....[77]

Meanwhile, with Love's help, the young Canseliet married Raymonde Caillard, a 19-year old Parisian girl who presented him with a son that very same year, one month after the death of his father. A divorce took place later on, and unfortunately, his son, Henri, died tragically seven years later from meningitis.

In the meantime, Fulcanelli, who up to that point had still not succeeded in obtaining the Philosopher's Stone, was labouring towards achieving the Great Work in the utmost secrecy in his Parisian retreat. Having completed the ultimate multiplication resulting from the great Coction in 1922, he decided to carry out the celebrated final transmutation of the base metal into gold, as Tradition demands. His success was undeniable, and he decided to renew the experiment in the presence of selected witnesses: his disciple, Eugène Canseliet, Jean-Julien Champagne, and a chemist friend, Gaston Sauvage, who worked at Rhône-Poulenc's.

The project took place at the Sarcelles gasworks in his disciple's room that had been converted into a modest laboratory, as mentioned earlier. And it was to the disciple that, under the Master's supervision, the realization was entrusted. The little chimney drew extremely well in that makeshift laboratory. Fulcanelli removed three tiny reddish fragments from a case, which Eugène Canseliet wrapped in wax and then threw into the molten lead in the crucible. A moment later, he cast the liquid into the ingot mould. The gold was magnificent! The transmutation was a complete success, and the young disciple was overcome with intense emotion, as can be easily imagined.

Some time after that, the Master withdrew. He chose to retire, in accordance with the Tradition perpetuated before him by numerous Adepts of the hermetic science.

---

[77] *Alchimie*, Eugène Canseliet, editions J. J. Pauvert, Paris.

## Fulcanelli's Manuscripts

A few months later, Fulcanelli apparently handed over three parcels sealed with wax to the disciple that he had so patiently trained for the preceding six years. These packages contained Fulcanelli's handwritten notes. Eugène Canseliet stated on that subject much later:

> Those were exquisite notes on sheets of paper in various formats. They were not written books.[78]

However, in actuality, those notes indeed represented the substance of three books by the Master, the respective titles of which were written on each parcel concerned. These were: *Le Mystère des Cathédrales, Les Demeures philosophales*, and *De Finis Gloriae Mundi*[79]. The disciple was given the task of formatting those notes and then editing them in literary form in order to produce the first book signed by Fulcanelli: *Le Mystère des Cathédrales*. Furthermore, he was instructed to write the introduction, sign it with his own name, and then add to his signature the three initials "F.C.H." for *Frère Chevalier d'Héliopolis*[80] - a designation which Canseliet was entitled to, even though he had not yet personally achieved the Great Work.

Given the enormity of the task before him, Canseliet was obliged to resign from his position at the Sarcelles gasworks. The conscientious disciple undertook to write on blank, unlined paper, and upon completion of his work, he submitted it via Jean-Julien Champagne to the Master, who expressed his approval and congratulated him. This was in 1922-1923, and the book appeared three years later, in 1926.

Eugène Canseliet then undertook to start work again. This time, with *Les Demeures philosophales,* which was an even more voluminous task since the text of it was twice as long as that of *Le Mystère des Cathédrales*. In the meantime - and again, through the

---

[78] *Le Feu du Soleil.*
[79] *The End of the Glory of the World.* (Tr.)
[80] Brother Knight of Heliopolis. (Tr.)

agency of Jean-Julien Champagne - the Master, whom Canseliet no longer met, instructed his disciple to return the text of *De Finis Gloriae Mundi* to him. Judging from his request, it is likely that the book contained certain revelations which Fulcanelli, after having thought them through in greater depth, realized the fullness of their gravity, and decided against publishing.

Further, we wish to warn the reader of these lines against any attempt - be it in the present or the future - to publish that text. It would be nothing more than a forgery, for almost all traces of the book in question have completely disappeared. Only a few notes allowing one to determine the outline of the book remain. They reappeared some sixty years later, shortly after the death of Fulcanelli's disciple (we can personally verify this statement. For further details, see "*Finis Gloriae Mundi – The End of the Glory of the World*" in Chapter 11). Indeed, never in his life did Eugène Canseliet ever leave room for doubt on this matter:

> It is only for *Finis Gloriae Mundi* that a few notes were actually written, and they were not included in the parcel with the other notes. I don't know why. I have used those texts, since they were outside, in order to get an idea of what that third book might have been like. What it would have been in actuality, I have no idea. But Fulcanelli wanted the parcel back and he took it from me. Perhaps there were very serious matters in there....[81]

The two texts that were published from these notes appeared in the second edition of *Le Mystère des Cathédrales* and in *Les Demeures philosophales*. They are the chapters dealing respectively with the cyclic cross of Hendaye and the paradox of the unlimited progress of sciences, including "Le Règne de l'Homme[82]", "Le Déluge[83]", "L'Atlantide[84]", "L'Embrasement[85]" and "L'Age d'Or[86]".

---

[81] *Le Feu du Soleil*, op. cit..
[82] The Reign of Man. (Tr.)
[83] The Flood. (Tr.)
[84] Atlantis. (Tr.)
[85] The Conflagration. (Tr.)
[86] The Golden Age. (Tr.)

Let us go back to the period immediately preceding the publication of *Le Mystère des Cathédrales*. At the beginning of the year 1925, the disciple and the Master's illustrator, Jean-Julien Champagne, moved into two garret rooms on the sixth floor at 59 bis rue de Rochechouart. Canseliet had again installed a small laboratory in his own room, which was, for the record, adjacent to the one occupied by the father of the famous violinist, Stéphane Grappelli. Jean-Julien Champagne also played that noble instrument - a successor of the *viola da braccio* - although doubtlessly with less virtuosity.

The following year, shortly after the publication of *Le Mystère des Cathédrales* in 1926, Pierre Dujols died at the age of 64.

> I greeted him sometimes (*said Eugène Canseliet*), when I caught a fleeting glimpse of him on his meager bed where he was lying stiff-jointed, suffering from arthrosis like Scarron. Consequently, he was unable to unbend his knees or leave the sitting position. So, in the evening when he was lying down, his knees remained at an angle and he used them as a writing stand.

The year after, Eugène Canseliet was presented with a daughter named Solange by his then 21-year-old companion, Germaine Hubat.

In 1930, when the disciple was still without news of Fulcanelli - and this for a very good reason, as we shall better understand a little further on - *Les Demeures philosophales* was published. Several years later, there were still unsold copies of the two books by the Adept who had remained anonymous, and who had certainly not made a fortune, to say the least!

### Evidence of the Precise Year of Fulcanelli's Disappearance

*Some Apparently Contradictory Statements*

We have read that, after the transmutation in 1922, Fulcanelli progressively retired and that from then on, Eugène Canseliet seemed to have had only more or less indirect contact with him. What should we make of that?

Eugène Canseliet tells us in his *Alchimiques Mémoires*:

Just a few days had passed after the death of Julien Champagne in his garret room at 59 bis rue de Rochechouart - a room which was quite identical to mine, although on the opposite side of the staircase that led to the corridor - when a coincidence that remains astounding occurred. This was the coming of the Sufi clergyman, diplomat and soldier [Mohtar Pasha], which transformed my modest life; a life that was already upset, *two years previously*, by the Master's accession to the "Absolute of Adeptship".[87]

As Julien Champagne died in 1932, this means that 'two years previously" was 1930. However, we are left wondering at the above statement given that Eugène Canseliet had alluded without doubt, in his preface to the *first* edition of *Le Mystère des Cathédrales*, dated October 1925, to the fact that the Master had already disappeared a long time before that:

> The author of this book is no longer *with us, and has not been for a long time*. The man faded away. Only his memory remains. I cannot without sorrow recall the image of that industrious and wise Master to whom I owe everything, and lament that he so soon departed. [...] His numerous friends, those unknown brothers who hoped to obtain from him the solution to the mysterious *Verbum dismissum* (missing Word) will join me in lamenting his loss.
>
> Could he, having reached the pinnacle of knowledge, refuse to obey the commands of Destiny? No man is a prophet in his own country. Perhaps this old saying gives the occult reason for the upheaval produced in the solitary and studious life of a philosopher by the flash of Revelation. Under the influence of that divine flame, the former man is entirely consumed. Name, family, native land, all the illusions, all the errors, all the vanities fall to dust. And, as with the phoenix of the poets, a new personality is reborn from the ashes. At least, that is how the philosophic Tradition would have it.
>
> My Master knew this. He disappeared when the fatal hour struck, when the Sign was accomplished. Who, then, would dare to set himself above the Law? [...]
>
> [...] Fulcanelli is no more. However, we have at least this consolation; that his thought remains, warm and vital, enshrined forever in these pages...

---

[87] *La Tourbe des Philosophes*, n°3.

## Evidence for the Actual Year of Fulcanelli's Departure

Furthermore, decisive and irrefutable evidence of the departure year was given to us when, thanks to a friend, we found an extremely important document. It goes without saying that no biography devoted to Fulcanelli or to his disciple has revealed this evidence up until now. This enabled us to definitely settle - and we are weighing our words carefully - that fundamental question.

In fact, this documentary evidence is an interview given by Eugène Canseliet to the French newspaper, *Le Figaro,* dated June 12-13, 1965. The article's title read: *Alchemists in the Atomic Era.... In his laboratory near Paris, an old man is obstinately pursuing the Quest of the Great Work,* and was written by Bernard Lesueur. We are reproducing here a copy - certified, of course - of a facsimile of this article.

What do we read in this article but the following, quite unequivocally stated:

> Spiritual heir to the very mysterious Fulcanelli, that other twentieth century alchemist, who died in 1923 - *officially* "dead", although for the Adepts, Fulcanelli - having achieved the Great Work - goes on living at our sides, but in a "parallel" universe.

Still though, how can we reconcile this with the contradictory assertion made by Eugène Canseliet regarding the year 1930? Let our reader be assured that we shall deal with this question very simply when the time comes, in subsequent chapters. The answer, it turns out, is self-explanatory!

It then only remains to provide evidence that any hypothesis formulated by any author regarding Fulcanelli's identity is incorrect if it does not concern an individual whose official death-certificate, **recorded in the civil status books, mentions the year 1923.**

## DES ALCHIMISTES A L'ÈRE ATOMIQUE...

### DANS SON LABORATOIRE, PRÈS DE PARIS

# Un vieil homme poursuit obstinément la "Quête du Grand Œuvre"

#### par Bernard LESUEUR

— Ce n'est donc pas une fable, il existe encore des alchimistes ?
— Bien sûr, j'en connais plusieurs qui, comme moi, consacrent toute leur vie à rechercher en laboratoire la pierre philosophale.
— La pierre, c'est, je crois, le résultat de ce que vous appelez le grand œuvre...
— ...Et le grand œuvre c'est exactement, ainsi que les anciens l'ont redit sans cesse, la répétition en laboratoire de l'œuvre des six jours dépeinte dans la Genèse.
— En fait, vous voulez créer un microcosme ?
— C'est très positivement, en effet, pour l'alchimiste, la création de son petit monde. A la base, une première matière est nécessaire qui est extraite de la mine, aussi pure que possible, et qui représente pour nous le chaos primordial.
— Et de ce « chaos », que cherchez-vous à tirer ?
— La pierre des philosophes ou « médecine universelle » qui, par sa perfection, sa subtilité rejoint l'Esprit même. Mais il faut se bien pénétrer que, pour la réussite de ce travail, une stricte discipline est nécessaire. L'alchimiste doit rester lui-même au diapason de la pureté dont il veut doter sa matière. Le Cosmopolite, un traité de 1669, précise d'ailleurs que les « scrutateurs de la nature doivent être vrays, simples, patiens, constans, pieux, craignans Dieu et ne nuisent aucunement à leur prochain ».
— Pour le commun, la pierre philosophale c'est pourtant, avant tout, la possibilité donnée à l'alchimiste de « fabriquer » de l'or.
— C'est en réalité qu'une de ses propriétés « secondaires ». J'ai moi-même participé à une

*L'alchimiste devant son fourneau : l' « Athanor », demeure du feu secret qui provoque toutes les métamorphoses...*

ALCHIMISTES, Frères de la Rose-Croix, Templiers, ces figures légendaires d'un passé oublié ont-elles vraiment disparu de notre monde « atomique » ?

Une crypte poussiéreuse. Surgissant ici et là de la pénombre : des cornues effilées, des vaisseaux de verre et d'étain, des fioles ventrues, de lourds mortiers de bronze, des pinces, des creusets. Au milieu de ce fatras, un vieil homme, dos voûté, visage creusé de rides, méditatif, éclairé par les flammes d'un antique fourneau. A cette image traditionnelle de l'alchimiste du Moyen Age, comparons celle d'un autre « souffleur », en l'an de grâce... 1965 !

A quelques kilomètres de Paris, dans un petit village de l'Oise, un homme de 65 ans, Eugène Canseliet, fils d'un maçon sculpteur, a aménagé son officine à l'intérieur d'une petite maison mi-normande mi-picarde. Depuis quarante ans, ce disciple de Nicolas Flamel, Basile Valentin et autres Paracelse, poursuit obstinément la quête du grand œu-

vre, de la fabuleuse pierre philosophale.

Un visage affable de bon grand-père, le front haut, coupé de rides, le cheveu rare, le nez chaussé de lunettes rondes, ce petit homme fait irrésistiblement penser à Pierre Larquey. Le type du modeste retraité. Mais dès qu'il parle « laboratoire » et « oratoire » — l'un et l'autre sont inséparables dans l'esprit du chercheur — ses yeux brillent, sa parole se précipite. Aucune ostentation toutefois. Pour lui, rien que de très naturel...

Si anachroniques que puissent paraître ses travaux, ce moderne « fils d'Hermès » ne se sent pas seul dans sa thébaïde. Des dizaines de lettres lui arrivent chaque semaine. Héritier spirituel du très mystérieux Fulcanelli, cet autre alchimiste du XXᵉ siècle mort en 1925 — « mort » officiellement car pour les Adeptes, Fulcanelli, ayant accompli le grand œuvre, continue de vivre à nos côtés mais dans un univers « parallèle » — Eugène Canseliet vient de préfacer la réédition, chez Jean-Jacques Pauvert, des traités hermétiques de son maître.

### Le mystère Fulcanelli

Nul n'a jamais pénétré le secret de la véritable identité de Fulcanelli, auteur hermétique du « Mystère des cathédrales » (1926) et des « Demeures philosophales » (1930). Certains ont voulu l'identifier à l'un de ses disciples : Julien Champagne, illustrateur de ses traités, ou même à... Eugène Canseliet. D'autres crurent voir en lui l'académicien J.-H. Rosny aîné, mort en 1940. Enfin, crédules ou fantaisistes ne craignirent point d'assurer que Fulcanelli n'était rien moins que... M. de Saint-Germain en personne !

Seul détenteur de la vérité, Eugène Canseliet s'est

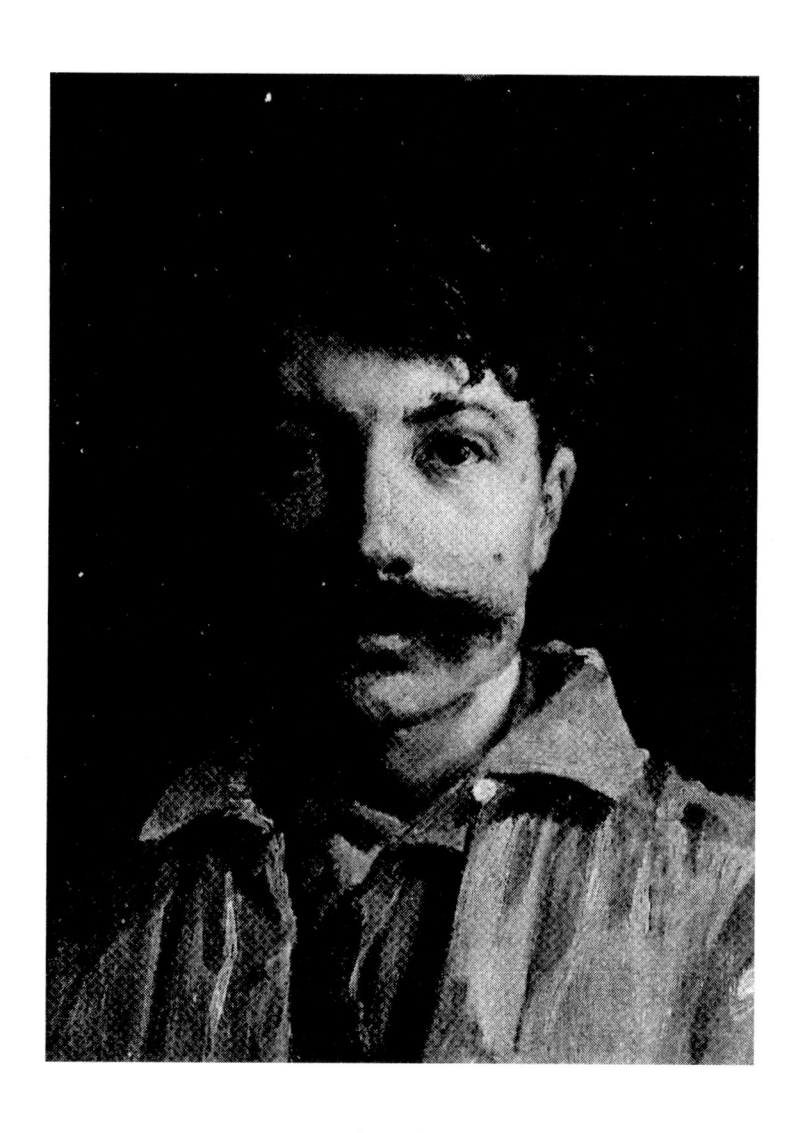

*Jean-Julien Champagne*

# V
# Who Was Jean-Julien Champagne?

What was the part actually played by this character who was brooding in the shadow of what can be called "*the Fulcanelli affair*"? Let us attempt to answer this question by analyzing the available biographical elements.

Jean-Julien Champagne was born in Levallois-Perret on January 23, 1877. Even as a child, it was already clear that he had a creative mind. Incredibly gifted at drawing, he matriculated at the age of 17 at the Paris School of Fine Arts, where he was a student of the painter Léon Gérôme. According to an article written by Robert Ambelain and published in the periodical *La Tour Saint-Jacques*[88], it would seem that Champagne already had a passion for alchemy in his adolescence. Again, according to Robert Ambelain, Champagne's sister, Renée Devaux (who lived in the Somme department), possessed photographs of a period in which we could admire the young Champagne surrounded by laboratory instruments of all sorts: retorts, a furnace, crucibles, etc. The young man was multi-talented, and in addition to drawing, he was also skilled in painting, music (he played the violin) and woodcarving. During this period of his life, he made a splendid clock representing a neo-gothic church. He also had a skilful hand for all things practical.

Soon after graduating from the Beaux-Arts in 1900, he began to pay frequent visits to the *Librairie du Merveilleux* bookshop where Pierre Dujols and his wife immediately took a liking to this young

---

[88] *Les Cahiers de la Tour Saint-Jacques*, IX, 1962 *The Tower of St. Jacques*. (Tr.)

man who was well read in hermetism and symbolic art. The erudite librarian opened his precious card-index cabinet for him, where he could draw at will. There Champagne also met a number of esotericists: Oswald Wirth, René Guénon (whose periodical, *La Gnose*[89], was being published by Pierre Dujols). One will recall that the learned librarian was also a fervent supporter of Grasset d'Orcet's "cabbalistic" theories and a well-versed Hellenist *who linked the origin of the French language to that of the Pelasgians* - all of which deeply interested the young painter-artist.

**Memorable Meetings**

Eugène Canseliet assured his readers in 1964 in his preface to *Le Mystère des Cathédrales* that Jean-Julien Champagne had met Fulcanelli in 1905, although the circumstances remain a mystery.

In 1907, Champagne became acquainted with the illustrious Ferdinand de Lesseps family whose residence - a sumptuous townhouse - was located on Montaigne Avenue in Paris. One of the sons, Bertrand, was well-versed in alchemy and a short while after meeting Champagne, he invited the young painter to work in a little laboratory installed in a house on rue Vernier, which was owned by his brother, Ferdinand-Jules. This was very close to rue Bélidor where, if we are to believe the *Voyages en Kaleidoscope*, the young hero - inventor Joël Joze - lived!

Officially, Champagne was employed by Bertrand de Lesseps to do industrial drawing and design a turbo-propeller. Unofficially, however (according to Robert Ambelain), he was working on discovering the secret of the alchemical Great Work in order to attempt to achieve it. It seems that Jean-Julien Champagne was entirely free to organize his work as he wished until the year 1917. He occasionally escaped for shorter or longer periods of time in order to do work for friends of Pierre Dujols, the booksellers-publishers Chacornac, who he had been recommended to by Dujols. Champagne's task here consisted of tracking old and rare books which specialized in occultism and were found in local libraries.

---

[89] *Gnosis*. (Tr.)

*Jean-Julian Champagne with his turbo-propeller*

This occasionally required him to travel in order to see and evaluate the books, and then make the appropriate selections.

Furthermore, in 1910, Fulcanelli employed him to carry out miscellaneous tasks and as a courier. This gave Eugène Canseliet an opportunity to meet them in Marseilles, surrounded by old alchemical writings penned by hands of the best authors. They were certainly not unknown to Pierre Dujols, who had spent his youth in Marseilles, and after completing his studies in a Jesuit college in Aix-en-Provence, had become a professional journalist. In fact, Jean-Julien Champagne was commuting between Paris and Marseilles since, as we recall, he was then working for the de Lesseps on a project developing a propeller for a screw-propelled sleigh, which we shall discuss in further detail later on. All of this was taking place on the background of the First World War, which had erupted a few months before.

As mentioned above, upon Bertrand de Lesseps' invitation, Jean-Julien Champagne was residing on Montaigne Avenue in order to work on his "screw propeller sleigh", where he received a regular remuneration in the form of rent. Champagne introduced young

Eugène Canseliet to the de Lesseps family who were acquainted with many people belonging to the worlds of politics, business, art and literature. The connections of the famed Ferdinand's descendents were very eclectic, to say the least. Politicians of various orientations could thus be seen in the sumptuous abode on Montaigne Avenue, as could Anatole France and the founder of the Surrealist movement, André Breton. Of course, it must be said that they were certainly not all invited to the same types of social evenings! It is at one such evening that the author of *Arcane 17* and *Nadja*[90] made the acquaintance of Eugène Canseliet[91]. This was the beginning of a long friendship that led to the sponsorship much later of the latter by the former at the *Société des Gens de Lettres de France*[92].

The author of the famous novel, *Voyages en kaleidoscope* - Irène Hillel-Erlanger - (the novel with real characters using fictitious names, which we discussed in Chapter 1) was also a regular visitor at the de Lesseps' home. In 1910, one of her close friends - either the young female alchemist, Louise Barbe, or the actress, Mrs. Roggers (wife of the writer, Claude Farrère, who authored, among other things, an odd novel on life prolongation, *La Maison des Hommes vivants*[93]) - was supposed to have modelled for Julien Champagne for a most evocative painting. The subject of the painting was *Le Vaisseau du Grand Oeuvre*[94] (no less!), in which the young, naked woman played the part of the philosopher's stone. She was decorated with thousands of blazing flames on a background rich in powerful alchemical symbolism[95]. However, although Grace's diamond sparkled and glittered on her forehead, she still evoked the same

---

[90] Cf. our preface entitled "André Breton ; 'soleil noir' et 'main de feu' ", of the excellent book by Richard Danier, *L'Hermétisme alchimique chez André Breton*, éditions Ramuel.

[91] See Eugène Canseliet's contribution to *Art magique* by André Breton ("Formes et Reflets") ("Shapes and Reflections").

[92] Society of Letters of France. (Tr.)

[93] *The House of Living Men* (Tr.).

[94] *The Vessel of the Great Work*. (Tr.)

[95] A representation of this painting is used as a frontispiece in the reprint of Eugène Canseliet's *Deux Logis alchimiques*.

erotic fascination as Countess Vera by her disturbing nakedness. Later on, André Breton was to confess to Eugène Canseliet that Paul Eluard, the poet of surrealism, was not indifferent to the charms and graces of Jean-Julien Champagne's model.

Furthermore, Champagne, who could occasionally be facetious, had found it amusing to play a prank on Louise Barbe's husband, Dr Voronoff. He once tampered with his father's identity card, assured Dr Voronoff that it was his own, and that he was born in 1854, but that he possessed the elixir of eternal youth which prevented him from ageing! We should add that Serge Voronoff was easily fooled by this, the more so since his research in the Collège de France laboratories was actually focused on rejuvenescence! Jean-Julien Champagne was, thus, rather whimsical and loved playing pranks.

Another example of this side of Champagne is found in a recollection by Eugène Canseliet at the end of his life in his article, *Alchimiques Mémoires*[96], about René Viviani who had formed a great friendship with the man he called his "Very Dear Fulcanelli":

> Having kept an incurable student-painter's mind, Julien-Champagne had a little dog he had named Jougy, whose hair was white and curled in large loops. He sometimes came accompanied by that friendly and funny animal. Her facetious master had her sitting very upright, and he ordered her to stand up, adding gravely: We are going to deliver our speech for Mr Viviani! Immediately, the little animal, a true busker, started giving grunts and growls that she modulated and emphasized with gestures of her forelegs, which she was in turn extending and flexing. Certainly, this was not distasteful, but having heard of that little number, Fulcanelli requested his illustrator not to have it played before the young de Lessepses, i.e. before the great-grandchildren of Ferdinand, the one who had contributed to the cutting of the Suez Canal, under Napoleon III.[97]

In a quite different context, let us remind the reader that Eugène Canseliet confided to André Breton that:

---

[96] *Alchemical Memories*. (Tr.)
[97] *La Tourbe des Philosophes*, 1982.

Of the various persons, all of a high standing, whom we saw around the Master at Montaigne Avenue, Raymond Roussel impressed us the most. And so much so that it appeared to us quite out of place that our old Julien Champagne could call that distinguished man "la classe"[98]. It is true that both men had belonged to the same contingent, the one of 1877, and that Mr Roussel, who had a passion for the internal combustion engine, had an admiration for the illustrator of Fulcanelli and Bertrand de Lesseps. It is also true that Champagne was the inventor of the screw-propeller sleigh for Ferdinand's eldest son that Raymond Roussel admired at Montaigne Avenue, and which he had photographs taken of.

Eugène Canseliet and Jean-Julien Champagne often paid visits to the latter's mother who lived at Arnouville-lès-Gonesse on *Viollet-le-Duc* Avenue, a street whose name is interestingly quite similar to Fulcanelli's own patronym. There they spent their time at their favourite artistic pursuit - painting - and during the summer of 1921, Eugène Canseliet painted a striking portrait of the friend he considered to be his master. An air of mystery exudes from the proud expression on the face framed by long, grey hair with hues of violet. Later on, Eugène Canseliet published a copy of this portrait in his *Alchimie expliquée sur ses Textes classiques* [99].

During the same year, Jean-Julien Champagne left Paris for Berry. Upon an invitation from the de Lessepses, he took up residence at their château de Leré, an estate which, although it was in Berry, was some ways from Bourges. There he was assigned the tasks of creating blueprints for a refrigerator and teaching drawing to young Paul. However, in that ancient dwelling that had once belonged to Agnès Sorel[100], the new landlord, Pierre de Lesseps, had installed a laboratory. And it seems that Champagne took the opportunity during his sojourn at the castle to devote himself to his passion - Alchemy - in his spare time.

Back in Paris the following year, he met Jules Boucher through one of his cousins[101] who was working with the latter at Rhône-

---

[98] The annual contingent of recruits. (Tr.)

[99] *Alchemy Explained by its Classic Texts*. (Tr.) éditions J.J. Pauvert, 1972

[100] Mistress of King Charles VII of France. (Tr.)

[101] A female cousin (Tr.).

Poulenc's. Jules Boucher was well-versed in esotericism, and in occultism in particular, and the two men immediately established very good relations. Then, in the fall of the same year, Fulcanelli invited Champagne to attend the famous alchemical transmutation carried out by Eugène Canseliet under Fulcanelli's direction. The chemist, Gaston Sauvage, was also present and served as a witness to the event.

During the course of the following year, it is known that the Master chose to progressively disappear. Jean-Julien Champagne returned to the castle in Leré, while Eugène Canseliet went on with his work in the small laboratory in Sarcelles until the day that Fulcanelli gave him the three famous wax-sealed envelopes that contained the documentary notes for Le Mystère des Cathédrales, Les Demeures philosophales, and Finis Gloriae Mundi.

Jean-Julien Champagne took the opportunity of his stay in the vicinity of Bourges to visit Jacques Coeur's palace and the Lallemant mansion, which aided him in the preparation of the illustration plates for Le Mystère des Cathédrales.

In the spring of 1925, he moved in with his friend, Eugène Canseliet, at 59 bis rue de Rochechouart in Paris. They resided on the same landing, each one in his own garret room. One day, they were both on their way to Montaigne Avenue to visit the de Lessepses when they again met the writer Raymond Roussel, who offered to bring them back home in the famous "screw-propeller sleigh", which had become quite operational:

> In the course of the year 1925, a great crowd gathered around the enormous automobile car that was greatly in the way of the street cars going and coming back on a single !ane.

At that time, Champagne was frequently seeing Jules Boucher[102], who thought that the Master's illustrator was Fulcanelli himself. The painter had doubtlessly boasted that Fulcanelli and himself were one and the same person during an evening when absinth (for which he had a particular fondness) had flowed rather abundantly. One is

---

[102] They already had met in Arnouville, where Jean-Julien Champagne sometimes stopped by.

already aware of how fond he was of jokes and pranks, and how whimsical he could be. Indeed, he had forged the handwriting and signature of Paul Le Cour, the renowned founder of the Atlantis association[103], in order to send a letter to the Director of the *Mercure de France*[104] magazine. In that letter, "Paul Le Cour" submitted to the Director, Mr Valette[105], a request to collect funds from readers with a view to erecting a memorial monument for the Martyrs of Atlantis "in the middle of the Sargasso Sea", which would naturally be "insubmersible and floating"! As one might imagine, that rather tasteless joke resulted in Paul Le Cour being severely reprimanded, and in the face of so much derision and cynicism, he had difficulties getting over it.

**Strange Company**

Jules Boucher, erroneously considering himself the disciple of Fulcanelli, then encouraged Champagne to associate with some rather sinister acquaintances, as we shall soon see. He introduced him to Alexandre Rouhier, a former market manager for a 'left-bank'[106] publishing house. This was the *Editions Véga*, which was attached to a bookshop of the same name. Rouhier was the author of a book entitled *De l'Architecture naturelle*[107] and had just finished writing an essay on the plant that 'makes astonished eyes': peyote. Additionally, our Doctor of Pharmacology was practising Satanism in the *Très Haut Lunaire*[108], or *Grand Lunaire* cult, in which he was an official. This cult met on nights of the full moon near the dolmen in the Meudon woods. Later, Eugène Canseliet stated:

---

[103] Whose objective was to collect all hermeneutic and archaeological data that might prove the existence and the probable location of mythical Atlantis.

[104] A very serious and prestigious literary magazine founded in Paris in 1724, and which existed until 1825. Rémy de Gourmont and Alfred Jarry, inspired by the name, founded a symbolistic periodical by the same name in 1890.

[105] Who not only managed the prestigious magazine, but also occasionally wrote articles for it.

[106] Left bank of the Seine River. The fashionable part of Paris. (Tr.)

[107] *On Natural Architecture.* (Tr.)

[108] Most High Moon-Dweller. (Tr.)

The most active ones were undoubtedly Alexandre Rouhier, Gaston Sauvage and Jules Boucher. The three of them more or less coaxed poor Julien Champagne into a less than commendable collaboration that alienated him forever from Fulcanelli's strong protection[109].

The above statement is of no little significance. In his book entitled *Sectes et Rites*[110], Pierre Geyraud wrote about the "Most High Moon-Dweller":

> In the third and last degree, initiates assemble in the main *occultum*, on rue Chapon, precisely in the Saint-Merri parish. The room is hung with red. The Baphomet grimaces behind red curtains. In a cage, toads, satanic beasts. There the supreme teachings are delivered, based on Fulcanelli's (*Le Mystère des Cathédrales*), Schwaller de Lubicz's (*Adam, l'Homme rouge*[111], Lotus de Pïni's (*La Magie et le Mystère de la Femme*[112]) and Crowley's books.

And as if this were not enough, Pierre Geyraud gives some specifics a few lines before:

> The Black Pope of the sect is, like the other officials, an alchemist. His assistants are a Left-Bank publisher, a renowned journalist, a banker, an illustrator-painter, two young women, and many others, but those are mere executives.

The protagonists in the "case" are easy to identify: the publisher, Alexandre Rouhier; the journalist, Jules Boucher; the illustrator-painter, Jean-Julien Champagne. As to the "Black Pope", how could we not guess that under his tunic was hiding Gaston Sauvage (a character appearing in P. N. de la Houssaye's novel) - the chemist who was one of the witnesses at the famous transmutation carried out in 1922 at the Sarcelles gasworks?

Quite enlightening! At any rate, Jules Boucher, who was later forced to have himself exorcised, admitted that he was at the same

---

[109] In *Le Feu du Soleil*.
[110] *Cults and Rites*, Editons Emile-Paul, Paris, 1954.
[111] *Adam, the Red Man*. (Tr.)
[112] *The Magic and the Mystery of Woman*. (Tr.)

time fascinated and terrified by the Rhône-Poulenc chemist, Gaston Sauvage[113] who did, in fact, bear quite a fitting name!

We have seen that Pierre Geyraud evokes not only the well-known luciferian and Satanist, Alistair Crowley, but also Fulcanelli, as being among those the sect considered as the inspiration for their ideas[114]. Here we must really wonder why, even if Julien Champagne had been partially responsible for this - in addition to esotericist, Schwaller de Lubicz, for his book *Adam l'Homme rouge*, about which we shall say more later on.

For the time being, let us keep in mind that *Jean-Julien Champagne knew Schwaller de Lubicz personally* as he had met him several times during his later years. This is according to a statement reported in Geneviève Dubois' book[115] by André Vandenbroeck, to whom Schwaller de Lubicz purportedly made confessions in 1959 at his house in Grasse.

Eugène Canseliet was aware of the relationship between Schwaller de Lubicz and Jean-Julien Champagne, but was not aware of everything. Indeed, a secret agreement had purportedly been made between the two men (this also according to André Vandenbroeck) that dealt with an extremely delicate task entrusted to Jean-Julien Champagne by the esotericist and Egyptologist, which that esotericist was subsidizing. This task was no less than penetrating the mystery of the blue and red dyes in the exceptional stained-glass windows of Chartres Cathedral! That the two men were successful in that task would be saying enough. However, Geneviève Dubois claims that the successful result of that experiment was reported by Eugène Canseliet himself in his second preface to *Le Mystère des Cathédrales*. This is entirely incorrect and the error is easily demonstrated. That letter was discovered by Eugène Canseliet after the disappearance of Fulcanelli and was addressed to the latter's *'initiator'*, rather than 'attributed to Fulcanelli's *master*', as Geneviève Dubois erroneously asserts.

---

[113] Savage (Tr.).
[114] "Maîtres à penser" in the original. (Tr.)
[115] Geneviève Dubois, *Fulcanelli dévoilé*, éditions Dervy, Paris, 1992.

Eugène Canseliet was very clear on this subject:

> Thus, the author of *Le Mystère des Cathédrales*, for many years, kept as a talisman the written proof of the triumph of his true initiator.[116]

And, the following is the ambiguous sentence that Geneviève Dubois interpreted as being the confession of the solution to the problem of red and blue dyes in the stained-glass windows at Chartres:

> [...] what comforts me in certainty is that the fire only dies out when the work is achieved and the whole tinctorial mass impregnates the glass which, from decantation to decantation, remains absolutely saturated and becomes luminous like the sun.[117]

The above, in fact, most certainly does *not* refer to an *archemical* process of dyeing glass, even if it is extraordinary in and of itself. It does, however, refer to the pure and sheer application of the penetration power (*ingrès*) of the philosophers' stone such as was described accurately by Fulcanelli himself in his *Demeures philosophales*. Apparently, this was entirely missed by Geneviève Dubois.

Further, she should have carried out her alchemical research more in depth prior to meditating on the following, unequivocal, lines:

> Above all, it is all important is to remember that the philosopher's stone appears to us in the shape of a crystalline, body, diaphanous, red in the mass, yellow after pulverisation, dense and quite fusible although fixed at any temperature, and which its inner qualities render incisive, fiery, penetrating, irreducible and uncalcinable. In addition it is soluble in molten glass...[118]

This is the undeniable evidence that the alchemist has obtained the stone and that transmutation can be achieved successfully!

It is quite obvious that the letter involved is not from the pen of Schwaller de Lubicz, as Geneviève Dubois would like us to believe, since it was not addressed to Champagne but, let us repeat it, to *Fulcanelli's initiator*!

---

[116] *Le Mystère des Cathédrales*, p. 17. *Mystery of the Cathedrals*, p. 10.
[117] Ibid. p. 18 (Fr.), p. 11 (Eng).
[118] Op. cit., T. I, p. 262. (Fr.), p. 137 (Eng).

In order to remove any doubt, the reader is referred to the text of this letter, which is given in the Appendix.

## Julien Champagne Poses as Fulcanelli

Let us come back to the "Fulcanellian" pretensions of Jean-Julien Champagne (the "stand-in") who, indeed, persisted in keeping up that pretence for the benefit of his pseudo-disciple, Jules Boucher. He even went so far as to dedicate a copy of *Le Mystère des Cathédrales* to him in the following eloquent terms:

> To my friend Jules Boucher, fervent adept of High Sciences, I offer this token of cordial affection. (*signed*) A.H.S. Fulcanelli[119].

The handwriting undoubtedly being Jean-Julien Champagne's, there is no doubt about the stratagem. Furthermore, it seems that Champagne attributed to himself older 'disciples' such as Max Roset and a certain Steiner, both of whom he claimed to have initiated into alchemy in the small laboratory owned by the de Lesseps on rue Vernier. The same held true for Schwaller de Lubicz, contrary to what Dubois thinks.

In any event, Eugène Canseliet seemed to be quite unaware at that time of the fact that Jules Boucher discretely claimed to be "Fulcanelli's" (i.e., Jean-Julien Champagne's) disciple. The author of *Deux logis alchimiques*[120], published in 1945, even went so far as to dedicate his book to Boucher in the following terms:

> To Jules Boucher, to the common friend of Champagne and myself, to the hermeticist who, better than anyone else, is able to properly appreciate Fulcanelli's occult personality. Quite cordially. (*signed*)
> E. Canseliet.

After which, Jules Boucher used this friendly dedication without hesitation to loudly proclaim that it was an implicit confession that Jean-Julien Champagne and Fulcanelli were one and the same person! In 1962, Robert Ambelain published an article in the magazine

---

[119] A.H.S. for *Apostolus Hermeticae Scientiae*, meaning Apostle of the Hermetic Science.
[120] *Two Alchemical Dwellings*. (Tr.)

*La Tour Saint-Jacques*[121] in which he supported the same argument. This inevitably led to a response from Eugène Canseliet. In his *réponse à un réquisitoire*[122] of the same issue of the magazine, he wrote:

> Better than anybody else indeed, he [*Jules Boucher*] was able to accurately assess Fulcanelli's secret personality, for the excellent reason that he often heard people talking about the Master, even though he never obtained the privilege to be introduced to him. [...]

> But let us come back to Jules Boucher, who soon reappeared in his true light with his various attempts to involve me in some of his usual hoaxes. One of those coarse jokes- intended for a certain individual by the name of Laviolette who brought to light all the machinations with supporting documents as evidence - resolutely took me away from that maniac, and from a left-bank bookseller-occultist, his guarded counsel and damned commensal.

But it was, in fact, in a letter dated May 7, 1963 and addressed to one Charles Art... published in L.M. Otero's book (see bibliography) that Robert Ambelain revealed his true thoughts. The letter is quite enlightening and removes any ambiguity about Jules Boucher, as can be understood from the following passages:

> My Dear Charles,

> [...] No, I never received a Fulcanelli file from Boucher! Mine was started before the war, as I have written. I have information (not all of it published...) that Boucher never mentioned! I own photographs he never saw. The reason? He would have been cross with me for that investigation and for what I had learned from it, about the others and "about him"....

> [...] Fulcanelli existed "under another name". He incorporated himself in Champagne for the time necessary to write his two books; the latter was the - likely unconscious - medium. That is why he was working at night...

> [...] This is why the drafts of these nocturnal works, in a handwriting other than his own, were never found after his death. Without a doubt destroyed as the work progressed...

---

[121] Article entitled: "Jean-Julien Champagne alias Fulcanelli".
[122] Reply to an indictment (Tr).

That said, after Pierre Dujols' death in April 1926, Champagne no longer hesitated in posing as Fulcanelli, even with Schwaller de Lubicz, with whom his ties had become closer and closer until the successful experiment in 1930 that resulted in the famous discovery of the blue and red dyes that constituted the mystery of the stained-glass windows in Chartres Cathedral.

After his return from the *Plan de Grasse* property belonging to Schwaller de Lubicz, Jean-Julien Champagne did not appear to be quite the same to his faithful friend, Eugène Canseliet. He immersed himself in long, philosophical meditations and undertook to renew some spagyric experiments on the small, round stove in his sparse and squalid attic on rue de Rochechouart.

With Eugène Canseliet's assistance, he busied himself developing an ointment and a plaster that they both wished to submit for clinical trials in hospitals. Was poor Jean-Julien Champagne already suspecting that an illness awaited him that would soon bring him down?

At the end of 1931, his left leg became horribly sore. He dragged it painfully until he was eventually forced to keep to his bed a few months later. In his bedroom, which was lit by a petroleum lamp whose beam he had adjusted with an attached lens, he sniffed galbanum[123] from a metal box he always kept at hand, and slowly sipped absinth to soothe the pain.

Eugène Canseliet tried to give him as much relief as he could by changing his bandages, but to no avail. The inflamed arterial blockage developed into gangrene, growing worse daily. At the break of dawn on August 26, 1932, Jean-Julien Champagne passed away in great poverty. He was 55 years old.

His sister, Renée Devaux, took the few papers he had left. Eugène Canseliet remained on excellent terms with her, as well as with her husband, who had acted as a go-between for his brother-in-law for a long time.

---

[123] A bitter, aromatic gum resin extracted from an Asiatic plant (Ferula galbaniflua) or any of several related plants and used in incense and medicinally as a counterirritant. (Tr.)

Jean-Julien Champagne was buried three days later in the cemetery at Arnouville-lès-Gonesse. A few months later, a marble slab was placed on his grave. It had been ordered by his sister, but had been paid for by Schwaller de Lubicz, who was also behind the composition of the epitaph:

> *Here lies*
> *Jean-Julien*
> *Champagne*
> *Apostolus Hermeticae Scientiae*
> *1877-1932*

A year and a half later, Eugène Canseliet happened upon Schwaller de Lubicz's book entitled, *Adam, l'Homme rouge*. After having read it carefully, he decided to write the author a letter, dated December 4, 1933, from which the following are excerpts:

Sir,

It may be that my name, written on the back cover, is not completely unknown to you since, having been very close to Mr Champagne in the last years of his life, you may have heard him talk about me sometimes. Since his death, I have been pursuing on my own the aim of our collaboration that started seventeen years ago, and which led us to rent two neighbouring attic rooms at 59 bis rue de Rochechouart in January of 1925.

It so happens that I was lucky enough to have been lent a very interesting book a few days ago - Adam, l'Homme rouge - which taught me something that our mutual friend had neglected to tell me - i.e., that you are the author of that curious and scholarly book. In it you demonstrate very deep knowledge and highly philosophical ideas about the primeval androgynous state - the same ones that were embraced by Mr Champagne after his return from Plan de Grasse, and which seemed to have overturned the notions he held before. As we both followed this new orientation, we went back to the study of the caput mortuum of the first work, which we had previously always rejected as useless and valueless scoria. [...]

Isn't it possible that Mr Champagne also showed an incomprehensible and surprising lack of memory towards this material part of your work, unless this was due to untimely discretion and excessive reserve?

Whatever the reason, I feel unable to rid myself of the painful impressions left in me by some unexpected events, some unsuspected facts, that took place at the end of his life and after his death, which gave rise to atrocious scenes of which I cannot say whether they were more loathsome or disturbing. It should be said that for a long time he was progressively under the deplorable influence of a woman. Alas! Narrow-minded persons too often exert such influence on superior minds.

But all of that is of no significance and has no other interest apart from the negligible one of the artificial things of this world. Quite different is the value I will give to the reply you will deem adequate to address me in order to provide me with clarification, in the proportion you deem useful, about the primary point of the great work. [...]

Eugène Canseliet

It seems that Eugène Canseliet had already foreseen what was going to happen more than half a century later with the publication of André Vandenbroeck's book, *Al-Kemi: A Memoir: Hermetic, Occult, Political and Private Aspects of R.A. Schwaller de Lubicz*[124]. Once again, Geneviève Dubois erroneously wrote that the author claimed in this book that Julien Champagne was Fulcanelli.

Jean Laplace exclaimed that it was Joscelyn Godwin who, one year later, in his English critique of the book published in the review, *Aries* (no.8), decided on his own accord to "put to death" the Fulcanelli myth by the following extrapolation:

Vandenbroeck, not finding this point important, did not dwell on that miserable man's identity. Aor's (Schwaller de Lubicz' nickname) anecdotes, however, leave no room for doubt about his identity: Jean-Julien Champagne, which, for many, will not be a surprise...

How could Geneviève Dubois endorse this, in contempt of any objectivity, when André Vandenbroeck had only written:

[...] The information about what Fulcanelli was doing was obtained from the Frères d'Héliopolis, in particular from Canseliet, Champagne ...

---

[124] Inner Traditions, 1987.

[...] I felt and I assured him of this, that to get a clear idea of the situation, History was in no need of an identification. [...] I swore to keep his name secret. I shall keep my promise.[125]

## The Much-Debated Identity of Fulcanelli

Eugène Canseliet had, in a veiled manner, attempted throughout his life to put the reader on the trail of Fulcanelli's identity. He did this by leaving behind many clues that would permit one to discern the true personality that dwells in the shadows of the Master's pseudonym. This naturally left the door open to several hypotheses, not all of which, alas, were without a certain degree of subjectivity or partial after-thought, to say the least. These shall be refuted further on. For the time being, let us simply make mention of them.

### Erroneous Hypotheses

To whom in Eugène Canseliet's entourage has Fulcanelli's true identity *not* been attributed? When Canseliet maintained, as he did from the start, that he was himself the disciple (and was thought to be so as well by Paul Le Cour, the founder of the *Atlantis* association), authors Jules Boucher, Robert Ambelain, Robert Amadou, and more recently, Geneviève Dubois, loudly proclaimed without hesitation that Fulcanelli could be none other than the painter, Julien Champagne, unless the latter had conned René Schwaller de Lubicz or Pierre Dujols.

Shortly after Eugène Canseliet's death, Robert Amadou published the results of a so-called investigation into Fulcanelli's identity in the columns of the magazine *L'Autre Monde*[126] - a piece pejoratively entitled, *"The Fulcanelli Affair"*. We will attempt to briefly summarize it in the following points:

In 1980, the English bookseller R.A. Gilbert wrote a laudatory note dedicated to Archibald Cockren's book, *Alchemy Rediscovered and Restored*, in which he made mention of "practical research by

---

[125] *Al-Kemi: A Memoir: Hermetic, Occult, Political and Private Aspects of R.A. Schwaller de Lubicz*, Inner Traditions, 1987.
[126] *The Other World*. (Tr.) (N°s 74, 75, 76)

the most famous of modern alchemists". Of course, this referred to Fulcanelli, about whom R.A. Gilbert confidently wrote:

> His real existence, contrary to the ones of mythical French Adepts, is beyond any doubt.

In the same year, a book entitled *The Fulcanelli Phenomenon*[127] was published in London. Its author, Kenneth Rayner Johnson, maintained (among other things that we shall refer to later on) that Fulcanelli had succeeded in achieving a metal transmutation at the Château de Leré near Bourges, in the presence of Pierre de Lesseps, two physicists, one chemist, and one geologist. Albert-Richard Riedel, better known under the name of *Frater Albertus* (*The Alchemist of the Rocky Mountains*), also asserted the same thing.

In a Doctorate thesis entitled, *L'Alchimie en France dans la première moitié du XXe siècle*[128] (1981), Pierre Pelvet identified Fulcanelli as F.J. Jollivet-Castelot, the "hyper-chemist" we talked about in a previous section. He did this, however, without formally rejecting the hypothesis by which Fulcanelli and his disciple, Eugène Canseliet, would have been one and the same person!

We note that a certain Robert Jolivet had been the Abbé of Mont-Saint-Michel in the XVth century. His crest, presented on the ramparts, figured at the end of the first edition of *Dwellings of the Philosophers*.

Writer Jacques Bergier, co-authoring with Louis Pauwels, wrote *Le Matin des Magiciens*[129] in which he reported the famous transmutation carried out by Fulcanelli in 1922. He maintained that he had met with Fulcanelli in 1937, and shortly prior to his death is said to have confessed to Robert Amadou that Fulcanelli was indeed Schwaller de Lubicz. The alleged meeting with Fulcanelli was said to have taken place in June of that year on the gasworks premises at place Saint-Georges in Paris. At that time, Jacques Bergier was close to Prof. André Helbronner who had founded a nuclear research laboratory. The man with whom Bergier met purportedly then declared:

---

[127] Publ.: Neville Spearman, Jersey
[128] *Alchemy in France in the First Half of the Twentieth Century.* (Tr.)
[129] *The Morning of the Magicians* (Tr.).

Coat of Arms of Robert Jolivet, on the wall at Mont-Saint-Michel and as used as the endpiece of the first edition of *Les Demeures philosophales*

> "Mr Helbronner, to whom you are, I think, the assistant, is in search of nuclear energy. Mr Helbronner was so kind as to keep me informed about some of the results obtained, among others, the presence of radioactivity corresponding to polonium, when a bismuth thread is blown by an electric discharge in high-pressure deuterium…"

This is followed by a cautionary sentence regarding the many dangers of radioactivity. He then added:

> "I know what you are going to say, but that is irrelevant. Alchemists did not know of the core's structure, did not know of electricity, had no detecting means available. Hence, they were unable to operate any transmutation. Hence, they never could release nuclear energy. I will not try to prove what I am going to tell you now, but I beg you to repeat it to Mr Helbronner: geometrical lay-outs of extremely pure materials suffice to trigger atomic forces without any need to use electricity nor vacuum techniques…"

And then, about the philosopher's stone and its applications:

"What is essential is not the transmutation of metals, but that of the transmutor himself. This is an ancient secret that, every century, several men find again. And what befalls them? Maybe one day I will know ..."

This is what Jacques Bergier confessed, and Bergier should have understood, from the words themselves of the man with whom he spoke, that he had not reached adeptship! It was then clear that this fellow could not have been Fulcanelli. In any case, the scientific writer remained particularly impressed by that unusual encounter, the details of which he somewhat modified in two subsequent publications: *Faire de l'Or* [130] and *Je ne suis pas une légende* [131] (1977).

Writer Robert Ambelain, author of a "Fulcanelli file" deposited with the Bibliothèque Nationale, as well as of an article published in the periodical *La Tour Saint-Jacques* [132], claimed that Fulcanelli was none other than Julien Champagne. He based his claim on the following three facts:

In 1926, bookseller-publisher Jean Schemit purportedly found very precise comments in the manuscript of the first edition of *Le Mystère des Cathédrales* about which Julien Champagne had previously talked to him;

Fulcanelli was supposed to have dedicated this book to Jules Boucher, preceding his pseudonym with the initials A.H.S., an abbreviation for *Apostolatus Hermeticae Scientiae* (Apostle of the Hermetic Science). This same title is engraved on the epitaph of Julien Champagne's tomb in the Arnouville-les-Gonesse churchyard. Hence, according to Ambelain, Julien Champagne and the person who wrote *Le Mystère des Cathédrales* could only be one and the same person.

The motto on the shield at the end of *Le Mystère des Cathédrales* is *uber campa agna*; where *campa agna* may phonetically designate Champagne, and *uber* was, according to him, one of Champagne's first names - Hubert - although he had always called himself Julien.

---

[130] *Making Gold* (Tr.).
[131] *I am not a Legend* (Tr.).
[132] *The Tower of St. Jacques.*

According to Robert Amadou, Eugène Canseliet and Fulcanelli could well be one and the same. "I believe, although I am not convinced nor certain, I repeat it, that Fulcanelli is Eugène Canseliet's pseudonym," he wrote. He was basing his assumption on Paul Le Cour's opinion, and on the fact that Pierre-Noël de la Houssaye - who knew Eugène Canseliet well, and considered him to be a genuine Adept, a *Brother-Knight of Heliopolis* - referred to him in his novel *L'Apparition d'Arsinoë*[133]. This is an excellent initiatory novel evidencing some alchemical knowledge in which Houssaye alluded to Canseliet's long manipulations near the fire of the athenor from which was extracted the *philosopher's gold*. Above all, Eugène Canseliet had admitted to him during the course of an interview published under the title *Le Feu du Soleil*[134] (éd. J. J. Pauvert, 1978), that he himself had written the text of *Le Mystère des Cathédrales* and of *Les Demeures philosophales* on the basis of notes given to him by Fulcanelli.

How could Robert Amadou not see in Pierre-Noël de la Houssaye's novel that the chemist with a university degree, the occultist and black magician described Gaston Sauvage rather than Eugène Canseliet?

Then Robert Amadou strangely denied the hypothesis about the criticisms attributed to Fulcanelli written in the margins of Stanislas de Guaïta's book *La Clef de la Magie Noire*[135], owned by Jules Boucher. After comparing that handwriting with handwriting of Julien Champagne, he observed their exact similarity and thus concluded that Champagne = Fulcanelli.

More recently, Richard Khaitzine, in his book, *Fulcanelli et le Cabaret du Chat Noir*[136], claims, after many a demonstration, that Fulcanelli was none other than Dr Alphonse Jobert, to whom we have already alluded. He argues that the presence of a silver hippocampus in the coat of arms at the end of *Le Mystère des Cathédrales* is all-important. He thinks he can make it out in the sign of the Montmartre Chat Noir cabaret referred to by Fulcanelli, and,

---

[133] *Arsinoah's Apparition* (Tr.)
[134] *Fire of the Sun*. (Tr.)
[135] *The Key to Black Magic* (Tr.).
[136] *Fulcanelli and the Black Cat Café*. (Tr.) éd. Ramuel, 1997

above all, he sees in it, in the manner of a rebus, the letter *J* to which only *aubert* has to be added - the argotic word for silver- to obtain *J aubert* = Jobert.

Furthermore, he reads the motto accompanying the shield not as *uber (campana agna)*, but as "ober ..."! Even more recently, he claimed Jobert was the mysterious "master" written about by Raymond Roussel, whom the latter nicknamed "Little Volcano".

*Geneviève Dubois' Regrettable Misconception*

If we use the word "misconception", it is quite on purpose, for that word refers to "getting it wrong", which on the whole is not dishonourable. Nevertheless, within this particular misconception is also the deep and scarcely veiled contempt in which the author holds *Fulcanellian* alchemy. The authors listed above had undoubtedly shown respect for Fulcanelli and had considered him an Adept of hermetic philosophy, which he masterfully discussed in both of his published books. However, Geneviève Dubois not only appears to hold contempt for *Fulcanellian* alchemy, but for Fulcanelli himself, who is also disparaged, run down and betrayed in such a manner that her book would have been more appropriately entitled, "*Fulcanelli dévoyé*[137]" rather than "*Fulcanelli dévoilé*[138]"!

"*L'Affaire Fulcanelli*"[139], another work by said author, is a fallacious and partial book full of glaring errors of logic, transcription and date. It is, as far as I know, a book that few noticed (with the exception of Jean Laplace), and one which ridicules and describes a hoax cunningly orchestrated by the duplicity of two document looters - Pierre Dujols and René Schwaller - and the ingenious ideas of Eugène Canseliet and his mentor Julien Champagne, in the manner of a novel by Flaubert: the "Bouvard and Pécuchet[140]" of the Belle Epoque. However, under the pretence of

---

[137] *Fulcanelli Undressed*! (Tr.)

[138] *Fulcanelli Unveiled*! (Tr.).

[139] *The Fulcanelli Affair*. (Tr.)

[140] *Bouvard et Pécuchet* is a novel about two old copists who decide to buy and run a property in the country, but all their undertakings fail and they finally decide to resume their copying jobs and thus produce a kind of encyclopaedia of human foolishness. (Tr.)

making amends, Geneviève Dubois wished to make it clear at the end of the perfidious book that she thinks that young Canseliet had been the sport of Champagne, who thoroughly manipulated him.

Jean Laplace, therefore, justly expressed his indignation in the diatribe he published in *La Tourbe des Philosophes*[141], N°s 36-37:

> [...] I was still very naïve to think that those "questers" had only in mind to put a name on a pseudonym; I realized after some time that some of them were only trying, under the cover of that so-called "quest", to destroy the hated image of Eugène Canseliet, whom they so detested. [...].
>
> The malevolence and intentional prejudice warned against by Eugène Canseliet, again produced a heap of nauseous nonsense entitled *Fulcanelli dévoilé*. Still, in his *Alchimie expliquée*, and on that same page 12, the philosopher foresaw that four centuries would not elapse, as in the case of Flamel, before his own life would be meticulously sifted through without any benevolence by yet another Villain.
>
> [...] The new accusatory document that appeared in November 1992 (*Fulcanelli dévoilé*) goes even farther, insinuating that there never was an Adept Fulcanelli, since all of that had been a hoax of which Eugène Canseliet was the victim, unless he was a stakeholder in it. The hatred for Eugène Canseliet that emanates from that distasteful book is all the more easily released as the only one able to give answers has been dead for about ten years now. Still, when one realizes that the author is not even able to correctly read the original copy of the philosopher's published letter - so enormous are the mistakes - one is allowed to seriously doubt her insight.

Not content with all that, Geneviève Dubois, who was at that time directing a line of alchemical writings for publisher Dervy, decided in 1995 to publish an odd book under the name of "Jean-François Gibert" entitled *Propos sur la Chrysopée, avec en annexe le Manuscrit de Pierre Dujols-Fulcanelli traitant de la pratique alchimique*[142], in which the author expresses, without beating around the bush, her negative intentions (p. 21):

---

[141] *The Philosopher's Peat.* (Tr.)

[142] *Remarks on the Chrysopée with an appendix of a manuscript by Pierre Dujols-Fulcanelli treating practical alchemy.* (Tr.)

Newton's case study now being almost completed, we will now talk about the case of Fulcanelli, one which is close to a hoax and represents the final form of pseudo-alchemical materialism, a blind alley in the hermetic labyrinth. To prove our statements we are going to present a still unheard of manuscript from Dujols-Fulcanelli on the Chrysopea. This will enable students of the philosophical art to get their own ideas on the Great Work considered in the manner of *Le Mystère des Cathédrales*, written from the notes left by Dujols and Champagne, by the scholarly blower, the late Eugène Canseliet.

What an edifying document, indeed, is this text which, while correctly reflecting Pierre Dujols' style, is at the perfect opposite of the alchemical path followed and recommended by Fulcanelli. We can assure the reader - on the word of a hermeticist - that the "Eagles or Sublimations" described by the learned bookseller were inevitably due to fail. Firstly, because the chosen *materia prima* - sulphide of lead reduced by means of iron - was most definitely not the one used by Fulcanelli. In addition, the nitre salt floating on the surface of the compost is certainly not used during the delicate, genuine sublimations in the Second Work, for which, it must be added, Pierre Dujols did not take into consideration the importance of the philosophical *"vytriol"* or of the *"adamic earth"*, which he apparently knows nothing about. His mistakes are, therefore, quite immense! Let us also add that he never alludes to Champagne in the above-mentioned text, in all probability because it was a question of his student L. Faugeron, who was not a very gifted beginner in alchemy.

Again, J. F. Gibert's "misconception" is to be envisaged here in the double etymological sense we referred to before. The truth is that most of Pierre Dujols' alchemical knowledge was speculative, and sometimes even erroneous, in spite of his *Hypotypose* to the *Mutus Liber*. A very learned person in matters esoteric in general, he was however very humble and would have easily recognized his own weaknesses in operative alchemy, if one is to judge by the following lines, which he wrote in his comment on François Cambriel's, *Cours de philosophie hermétique et d'alchimie*[143]:

---

[143] *A Course in Hermetic Philosophy and Alchemy.* (Tr.)

Indeed, it is always through mysterious ways that the true elected ones are recruited by the Invisible, as this was evidenced at the place of *one of our friends, a true Adept* of modern times, who obtained philosophal gold of which we possess an interesting fragment....

Was he talking about his friend, the Adept Fulcanelli? It is at least permitted to think that he was.

## A Monument to Subjectivity

The book *Monument to the End of Time*[144], subtitled *Alchemy, Fulcanelli, and the Great Cross*, by the American team of Jay Weidner and Vincent Bridges, presents a different problem. Weidner and Bridges, unlike Mme Dubois, have the insight to realize that Fulcanelli was a real person, and their enthusiasm indicates that they understand that his work is important. Unfortunately, they do not appear to quite understand what that work is. This could be due to the fact that they do not have access to the broader research that is only available in French.

As an example of whether they understand what the great Alchemist really meant, they go so far as to suggest that the work *The Architecture of Nature*[145], published in 1943 during the height of the Second World War, could be the third volume by Fulcanelli, *Finis gloriae mundi*! In it, they smell "a whiff of the authentic voice, the Fulcanelli of *Le Mystère*". Why do they specify *Le Mystère*? Because they have been 'disappointed' by the Master's second tome, *Dwellings of the Philosophers*, a book they say "is uneven, without the internal coherence and brilliant symbolic by-play found in *Le Mystère*.... The voice that seemed to know so much in *Le Mystère* is here hesitant and unclear."[146]

The problem with symbols is that they offer different interpretations to different viewers depending on what is within the viewer. We suggest a simple explanation for the disappointment

---

[144] Weidner, Jay and Vincent Bridges, *Monument to the End of Time: Alchemy, Fulcanelli, and the Great Cross*. Aethyrea Books, LLC, Mount Gilead, N.C. 1999.
[145] Ibid, pp. 25-26.
[146] Ibid, p. 25.

sprung from the apparent discrepancy: that if they believe the symbolism of the two works is so different and utterly lacking in the second book, perhaps our two American friends have completely misunderstood the symbolism of the first volume, the one they praise so highly. Their decoding of the Cross at Hendaye illustrates this point, for one would be stretching symbolic interpretation to the point of pure subjectivity to claim any references in Fulcanelli to the Cube of Space! They end up rejecting one book, *Dwellings*, that is known to be by the Adept and associate him with a book with which he had nothing to do! True alchemists recognize in *Dwellings of the Philosophers* a book rich in its descriptions of the Great Work.

As to the identity of the Adept, their forensic expertise leads them to speculate that he may have been "an immortal or very long lived individual"[147] perhaps living for two hundred years, because "an in-depth textual analysis of *Le Mystère des Cathédrals* reveals evidence that Fulcanelli was born and educated in the 18$^{th}$ century"[148]! We leave the reader to follow the implications of such an in-depth analysis and consider what this might suggest about the validity of the rest of their interpretation.

Before returning to our own investigation, we cannot let pass their characterization of the faithful student, Eugène Canseliet, as "a young occult upstart"[149]!

Nevertheless, again we note their insight and enthusiasm for Fulcanelli which is encouraging. But, to use an American phrase to describe the end result: "With friends like this, who needs enemies?"

---

[147] Ibid, p. 242.
[148] Ibid, p. 237.
[149] Ibid, p. 21.

# VI
# These Men of the Institute and Alchemy

According to Eugène Canseliet, Jean-Julien Champagne was Fulcanelli's *illustrator*, which - according to the etymology of the word - means the one that made the Master "illustrious", who "gave light" to him (*lustrare*), or who brought him "into the light" (from Latin *illustris*, "luminous"). In any event, it is the painter's name that was used to register the copyright of Le *Mystère des Cathédrales* at the Bibiothèque Nationale in Paris prior to the original publication of the book by Jean Schemit in 1926. Afterwards, Eugène Canseliet's name was associated with Fulcanelli for the successive publications of both his books by, among others, Jean-Jacques Pauvert[150]. In the above-mentioned article, published in *La Tour Saint-Jacques*[151], Eugène Canseliet gave the following explanation:

> [...] I assert that the texts and drawings in *Le Mystère des Cathédrales* and *Les Demeures philosophales* are my full and sole property, that I am the only one named in the agreements made and signed with Jean Schemit - the first one on April 6, 1926, the second one on November 6, 1929, and this when Jean-Julien Champagne was still alive; for he died, as it is known, on August 26, 1932. That is undoubtedly clear, neat and undeniable, and will nip any dispute in the bud, whatever it may be about, and wherever it may come from, since it goes without saying that I am in possession of both holographic and justifying documents.
>
> Thus, while securing his continuous anonymity, Fulcanelli did sooner or later envisage for my benefit - perhaps as a reward for the long

---

[150] See the first cover of *L'Alchimie expliquée sur ses textes classiques*, Eugène Canseliet.

[151] *The Tower of St. Jacques*. (Tr.)

discipleship effort that was promised to me - a second edition, which this time included the copyrights, contrary to the first one that was devoid of them, following the author's express will...

## Was Fulcanelli a Famous Scientist?

This question having been settled (contrary to Robert Ambelain's allegations in the same issue of *La Tour Saint-Jacques*. See previous chapter.), let us re-examine another statement made by Eugène Canseliet, this one concerning Fulcanelli's prestigious connections. On the back cover of *Les Demeures philosophales,* one finds the following text:

> If, in Heliopolis, I personally always feel - and quite intensely so - pledged by my oath to the ancestral discipline of the secret, how many free, high-ranking and powerful persons exist who might have been able to talk, even in confidentiality, but kept silent as if bound by some tacit agreement! It is important in particular to be aware that, in his youth, Fulcanelli was received by Chevreul, de Lesseps and Grasset d'Orcet; that he was Berthelot's friend, and that he knew Curie very well, who was his junior by twenty years....

And Eugène Canseliet added, in his *Alchimiques Souvenirs* (*La Tourbe des Philosophes*) that Fulcanelli was "too much of a laboratory man" to take any interest in or have any taste for occultism in general, as could at first be supposed.

Thus, with the exception of the illustrious Ferdinand de Lesseps and the original cryptologist, Grasset d'Orcet, the other names quoted were those of very high-ranking scientists, all of them members of the Institute. If Fulcanelli did indeed somehow associate with them, would this then not leave one with the understanding that he was a high-ranking scientist himself, and even perhaps a member of the Academy of Sciences? Or at least that he might have submitted some memoranda there about his own experimental theories?

If one questions the validity of this statement, given how daring it may appear, one should refer to the second book by the Master. Here, Fulcanelli bravely declared in what can be considered a confession that he did indeed belong to the scientific community:

François-Vincent Raspail was a confirmed alchemist and the works of classical philosophers were numerous among his other books. Ernest Bosc said that Auguste Cahours, a member of the Academy of Sciences, had told him that his revered master, Chevreul, professed the greatest esteem for our old alchemists. As a consequence, his library contained practically all of the significant writings of the hermetic philosophers.

[…] one of the most celebrated in chemical science, Marcellin Berthelot, did not merely adopt the School's opinions. Contrary to many of his colleagues who boldly talked about alchemy without knowing anything about it, he devoted more than twenty years to the patient study of original Greek and Arab texts. And from that long relationship with the ancient masters, the conviction arose within him that, "hermetic principles are, overall, as sustainable as any of the best modern theories".

[…]Were we not committed by the pledge we made toward them, we might add to [*the list of*] those scholars the names of certain leading scientific personalities who are entirely converted to the Hermetic Art, but whose very position obliges them to practice only secretly [152] …

The Master's avowal here is obvious. How indeed could Fulcanelli have been more eloquent as to the actual identity of his civil status?

The old scholar, Eugène Chevreul, who died at the age of 103, had a passion for alchemical texts. If we are to believe Auguste Cahours, Chevreul learned a great deal from these texts, and they were responsible for some of his discoveries in chemistry. His vast alchemical library was, in fact, bequeathed to the Natural History Museum. Further, Eugène Canseliet himself did not hesitate to state that Chevreul had advanced "quite far" on the hermetic path.[153]

It is true that his *Memoires* (more than eight hundred pages) deposited at the Academy of Sciences, as well as the books[154] he authored, show a deep understanding of alchemical philosophy as

---

[152] Emphasis ours.

[153] In *Le Feu du Soleil*. (Tr.)

[154] Although his books were more devoted to fatty compounds and vegetal dyes, resulting in his obtaining the position of Director of Dyes in the prestigious Gobelins factory, entrusted to him by Louis XVIII.

*Michel-Eugène Chevreul*
*(after a drawing by Maurin)*

applied to the mineral realm. This understanding is illustrated in the following lines:

> What was the basis of alchemy? The idea of the fermentation of bread. Wheat flour reduced to a dough by the addition of water and left to itself gets warm, puffs up - in a word, raises - and the dough thus raised up and warmed results in risen bread, showing holes within called 'eyes'.
>
> However, had the prepared dough been heated shortly afterwards, one would have obtained a quite compact azyeme bread. What does "azyeme bread" mean? Bread prepared without leaven. And what is this leaven (ζυμη)? It is leavened dough, fermented and called ferment because it had been observed that by blending it with flour kneaded with water, the mixture rises a few hours after its preparation when left in an adequately warm place.
>
> Let us come back to the alchemists focusing their attention on those phenomena. They had told themselves: since leaven has the property to change wheat dough into its own substance, let us take the appropriate materials, let us prepare a leaven that we shall call the philosopher's stone and which, like dough leaven, will change imperfect metals into silver and gold, an idea quite congruent with what can be read in a purported letter from Isis to her son Horus: "Remember" she says, "that man generates man, lion generates lion, and dog generates dog; likewise, gold generates gold."[155]

---

[155] *Summary of A History of Matter*, first article. (Tr.)

In his second article, the "dean of French students", as he modestly liked to refer to himself, added about transmutation:

> [...] thus the latter rested upon fermentation, the consequence of which was that with a finite quantity of philosopher's stone, one could transmute indefinite quantities of imperfect metals into a perfect metal. [...]

The alchemist added that the ferment he was preparing had the ability to transmute imperfect metals into their own substances, but that the most ancient alchemists were silent about the gold or silver that was necessary to introduce into the philosopher's stone.

Some of Eugène Chevreul's peers disputed his "encyclopaedic" work and reproached him for his *Histoire des Connaissances chimiques*[156] because they thought that he was too accommodating towards alchemy. His defence, which appeared in a memorandum to the Academy of Sciences on April 2, 1867, tells us a great deal about the old scholar's concerns:

> Certainly, if this work only concerned me alone, what is said about it would be of little concern to me. However, there exists an interested publisher, and it is on his behalf that I disapprove of a premature judgement or an ill-willed action, the consequences of which have been: 1) to interrupt the printing of the second volume devoted to the history of ancient people and the Middle Ages, seen in the light of chemistry; 2) to interrupt the printing of a third volume devoted to an overview of occult sciences, including alchemy....

And he concludes:

> I may, alas, produce a bad book; but thank God the reproach of having given it an untrue title cannot touch me...

It is true that his study was particularly objective, as can be concluded from the following sentence:

> Does alchemy present something scientific? I mean, can its truth be demonstrated? No! An answer that does not mean that alchemists have discovered nothing new.

---

[156] *A History of Chemical Knowledge*. (Tr.)

Fulcanelli reiterated Chevreul's views on this particular point when he wrote:

> Can we show evidence of atomic transformations affecting some molecules of a substance? How can their absolute value be recognized if they can only be controlled indirectly, in roundabout ways? Is that a mere concession made by moderns to the ancients? But we have never heard that hermetic science ever had to beg. We know it is rich enough in observations, well provided for in positive facts, not to be obliged to become a beggar.[157]

Doubtlessly, both our Adept and the old scholar Chevreul had read Louis Figuier, Doctor of Medicine, Doctor of Sciences, Master of Chemistry, and prominent author of *L'Alchimie et les Alchimistes*[158] (1854), a book in which he not only explained the trials and vicissitudes of the ancients and their doctrines, but also gave a history of transmutations from a rationalistic point of view. Fulcanelli himself reminds us of the difficulty for a scientist - as he himself was, which he implicitly admits here again - on the path that must be followed before apprehending the alchemical reality:

> Guard against using in your observations what you think you know, for you will be led to conclude it would have been better to have learned nothing rather than having to "un-learn" everything.
>
> This is, perhaps, superfluous advice, because achieving it requires the use of a tenacious will, which the mediocre are unable to exert. We know what it costs to exchange degrees, seals and scrolls for the humble cloak of the philosopher. We had to empty the chalice containing that bitter beverage at the age of 24. With wounded heart, ashamed of the errors made in our youth, we were obliged to burn books and notebooks, to admit to our ignorance and, a modest neophyte, to decipher another science on the benches of another school....[159]

The writings of old Chevreul and Marcellin Berthelot on Alexandrian alchemy, in addition to an association with these two eminent scholars, undoubtedly influenced Fulcanelli on his quest for the "Science of Hermes". Likewise, the meeting with the future

---

[157] *Les Demeures philosophales*, Vol. I.
[158] *Alchemy and Alchemists*. (Tr.)
[159] *Les Demeures philosophales* (Tr.)

permanent secretary of the Academy of Sciences, Jean-Baptiste Dumas, was certainly a determining moment for the young Fulcanelli. Let us not forget that the illustrious chemist wrote in his *Leçons sur la philosophie chimique*[160]:

> Would it be permitted to admit to isomeric simple elements? This question is closely related to the transmutation of metals. Positively solved, it would mean some chances of success in the search for the philosopher's stone...

Furthermore, Jean-Baptiste Dumas (1800-1884) examined *alchemical* and *archemical* processes in depth in his noteworthy *Traité de Chimie appliquée aux Arts*[161], which primarily dealt with dyeing enamel, glass and faience using metallic oxides, although those "lesser arts" were always considered to be intimately connected to the alchemical coction.

*Jean-Baptiste Dumas*

We will also recall that, according to Eugène Canseliet, Fulcanelli was well acquainted with Pierre Curie, the famous physicist, chemist, and member of the Institute, who was also deeply interested in alchemy:

---

[160] *Lessons on Chemical Philosophy*. (Tr.)
[161] *Treatise on Chemistry Applied to Arts*. (Tr.)

The conversations I heard in Fulcanelli's entourage left no doubt in this respect.[162]

He even went so far as to claim that:

> Curie [*Pierre*] was searching for the philosopher's stone in rare Soils. Curie's point, establishing the caloric degree above which ferromagnetic bodies reach a paramagnetic state, is quite representative of the alchemical orientation of that scientist's works...[163]

Moreover, Eugène Canseliet said that Fulcanelli possessed laboratory equipment that had been owned by his friend, Pierre Curie:

> In 1975. the little exhibition at the *Librairie du Merveilleux* on rue Condorcet, for which I supplied exhibits, included utensils that had belonged to Pierre Curie, which had passed on to Fulcanelli, and that the latter had offered to me.[164]

### The Mysterious "Mr Violette"

In light of the above, we may justifiably ask: is it possible to try and place Fulcanelli among the members of the prestigious Academy of Sciences, or at least among those scientists whose memoranda submitted to the Institut de France were retained, hence published?

At the same time, considering these many significant clues left like pebbles in the forest for the serious seeker, it would not be out of place to seek him among the eminent chemists, or perhaps physicists, of his time.

One will remember the repeated references made by Eugène Canseliet to a certain *Ch. Violette*, among others, in his preface to the *Mutus Liber*, in which he *associated* the patronym with Fulcanelli's real identity:

> Among all those assumed names and titles, those of Joseph Duchêne, Mr de la Violette, esq., seem to be *close* to the philosophico-humanistic identity of our author (Fulcanelli), even if his *personality proved to be very different* and was, in great part, that of a *spagyrist*.

---

[162] *Le Feu du Soleil*, p. 63.

[163] *L'Alchimie expliquée sur ses Textes classiques*, p. 287.

[164] *Le Feu du Soleil*.

There was, indeed, a chemist by that name who lived during the period in question. Charles Violette was a professor of chemistry at the Faculty of Sciences in Lille. He would later become the dean. He submitted several memoranda to the Academy of Sciences where they were crowned with success. The same held true for his work demonstrating the existence of "selenium in commercial copper, imported from Chile, and the cause for water acidity in organic analyses", his work "on resins that acquire new properties under the double influence of heat and pressure", "on mercury distillation by overheated water vapour, documented by the design of an appliance permitting to distil one ton of silver amalgam per day", "on potassium chloride sucrate", "on hydrogenous gas purification", "on the causes of oversaturated saline-solutions crystallisation", as well as "on the normal presence and dissemination of sulphate of soda in the air", "on the quantitative analysis of organic nitrogen through the Kjeldahl method", "on determining the ratio between real ashes and sulphated ashes in sugar-industry products", etc.

Before retiring, he showed a particular interest in the analysis of vegetal and animal fats, and notably "butters".

His pupil, who became his associate and then successor to the professorship in industrial chemistry at the Faculty of Sciences in Lille, wrote about him:

> How many happy hours I spent in his laboratory on rue des Fleurs; Violette knew how to make work pleasant. He was famous for his good mood. He was good, benevolent, even fatherly with his students. And he had a talent for making one fond of chemistry. His were unique lessons for their clarity and the elegance of their form.
>
> This is how he trained a whole generation of chemists. How many young people there are who, after having worked in his laboratory, owe to him a brilliant position in teaching or in industry![165]

It would be tempting, to say the least, in view of the eminent chemist's personality and work, to associate him with the pseudonym of Fulcanelli. However, Violette was born on June 14,

---

[165] Speech by Mr Buisine.

1823, and was therefore more than fifteen years older than our enigmatic Adept!

For the same reasons, it was necessary to exclude other "fulcanellisable" homonyms such as J.H.M. Violette, a professor of chemistry at the *Conservatoire national des Arts et Métiers*[166], who was in charge of "powders and saltpeters" and the author of a renowned *Dictionnaire des Analyses chimiques*[167] published in 1851 (Fulcanelli was then about ten years old), as well as Jules Viollet, author of *Fourneaux fumivores*[168], an essay published in 1860 and which our Adept would not have been able to write at the age of 20.

There is another track currently circulating on the Internet. It is the hypothesis put forward by Frédéric Courjeaud in a thrilling book where the author tries to demonstrate that Fulcanelli was the scientist-astronomer, Camille Flammarion[169]! In fact, the author of *L'Astronomie populaire*[170] was born in 1842 and thus corresponds to the age prerequisite. The eminent scientist, an astronomer by trade, also had a passion for occultism since his adolescence. Interested in the medium phenomena linked to spiritism (quite in fashion at that time), he authored a short essay in 1865 on the subject under the nom de plume of "Fulgence-Marion", which he also used to sign several books on various subjects from "balloon travelling" to the "marvels of vegetation". According to Frédéric Courjeaud, since *Fulgence* suggests fire or *flames*, one could read in the "Fulgence-Marion" alias the patronym of Flammarion.

This was then only one step away from using the phonetic Cabbala to associate the name of the famous astronomer with that of Fulcanelli, and the author doesn't hesitate to take that plunge. He suggested that "*Flamme d'Orion*[171]" was connected to Flammarion and Fulcanelli, since that constellation is surrounded by a gigantic,

---

[166] The National Conversatory of Arts and Trades. (Tr.)
[167] *Dictionary of Chemical Analyses*. (Tr.)
[168] Smokeless furnaces (Tr.).
[169] Frédéric Courjeaud, *Fulcanelli, une identité révélée* (*Fulcanelli, An Identity Revealed*), éditions Claire Vigne, Paris, 1996.
[170] *Popular Astronomy*. (Tr.)
[171] Orion's flame (Tr.).

incandescent nebula resembling a flame. He then divided Fulcanelli into Vulcan-Helios (The Sun's Fire) and Flammarion into Flamme-Arion (or Orion), thus designating the "Flame of Orion" under the pretext that Orion could be assimilated to the Sun. Then, a long list of cabbalistic proofs was given to support this assumption, even going so far as seeing in the initials F.C.H. "Flammarion-Camille-Hermès", in view of the famous astronomer's very first nom de plume.

A truly attractive theory, but then *the name Violette disappears* from the horizon. We should also not forget that Camille Flammarion died in 1925, the very year when Engène Canseliet wrote the first preface to *Le Mystère des Cathédrales*, which opened with the following lines that should be remembered here:

> "For a long time now the author of this book has not been among us. The man has disappeared...[....] Fulcanelli is no more. But we have at least this consolation, that his thought remains, warm and vital, enshrined forever in these pages."

So, what are we to think of all that, other than that we must base our investigation on something else!

# VII
# The Master's "Coat of Arms"

In a previous book[172], we already analyzed the *closing crest* at the end of *Le Mystère des Cathédrales,* the anagram of which (except for one letter) designates:

F-U-L-C-A-N-E-L-L-I!

Eugène Canseliet gives the following heraldic interpretation:

Sur champ de gueules, cette céréale [un épi de blé] surmontant l'hippocampe, tous deux d'or et issuant de champagne[173] de meme.[174]

On a field of gules, this cereal [an ear of wheat] tops a hippocampus, both of gold and issuing from the champagne [lower third of the coat of arms].

---

[172] Cf. Patrick Rivière, *Alchimie : Science et Mystique.*
[173] The "champagne" is known in heraldry as the bottom third of the coat of arms.
[174] We have left the original French, as well as included a translation, because the cabalistic analysis below is based upon the sounds of the French words. (Tr.)

Let us briefly examine the symbolic wealth of elements on this curious "coat of arms". In the first place, we notice that the hippocampus is etymologically related to the Greek καμπε *kampé* and to the Latin *campae* (meaning "by-ways", "ways out" according to the Gaffiot dictionary[175].). The sea-horse (*hippos, campos* in Greek) logically designates a *mare* ("*cavale*" in French), the hermetic *Cabala*, travelling through the "philosophers' sea" (in French: *la mer des philosophes,* their *mercury*).

Doesn't Victor Enile Michelet describe the scene in Canto XXVI of *The Odyssey* thusly:

There was the land horse leading the living and the sea horse leading the dead when, under the guidance of the psychopomp, Mercury, holding his golden staff, they must cross the currents of the celestial Ocean, the great spiritual waters mentioned in Genesis and in all other cosmogonies as well.

Moreover, as written by Louis Charbonneau-Lassay in his *Bestiare du Christ*[176], the ancient East considered the sea-horse to be a symbol for medical genius. Dioscorides, Galieni and Pliny assured us that the hippocampus had the power to discard or heal all human diseases. Galieni and Aetius considered it to be the symbol of divine Light.

In addition, the hippocampus has the following peculiarity: it is *the male that bears the impregnated eggs*, which require absolute darkness in order to hatch. The young sea-horses, having reached their time, are then set free and swim up towards the surface of the water. We then recall Fulcanelli's peremptory references to the necessity for absolute darkness - that is, the *nostoc*, which is related to *noctis* (night) - for the elaboration of the Work, and more precisely, for the bringing to life of the *dolphin* or "mineral embryo" on the surface of the *mercurial* bath upon completion of the delicate "sublimations of the Second Work". Sulphur or the germ of the philosophic gold then rises up to the surface of the bath. It is therefore not accidental that the heraldic field is "*or and gules*" (gold and red)!

---

[175] A well known Latin-French dictionary (Tr.).
[176] Bestiary of Christ. (Tr.)

As for the ear of wheat, it is obviously slang for *gold*[177]. The first word in the motto - *Uber* - means "fertile ground" in Latin, while *agna* in Latin is the young ewe of the alchemical bestiary, which symbolises the *prima materia*. Looking again at the ear of wheat, it suggests a cross of Lorraine, which in alchemy represents the precious saline ash indispensable to the Second Work. Finally, as far as the equal-branched cross formed by the openings in the shield's helmet is concerned, it of course indicates the alchemical crucible (*crux*) in which matter must be placed while undergoing all the triturations.

*Uber* (an anagram) should then be thought of as "rebus", and the coat of arms should be read as such!

According to Robert Ambelain (see the article mentioned above), the motto *Uber Campa Agna* quite naturally designates Champagne, whose first name would be his father's - Hubert - a name that appears after 'Jean-Julien' on the formal death-certificate, and one his sister used in the correspondence exchanged with Schwaller de Lubicz. In any case, there was indeed nothing to prevent Fulcanelli's illustrator from concluding his work with a final drawing, which included an ambiguous (to say the least) motto, while the principle of phonetic assonance, well known to those who have mastered the *language of the birds*, contributed even further to the legend!

In addition, it is unusual to note that for hermeticists the hippocampus is a synonym of the Egyptian *"god Amon's cornucopia"*, and that they designated their *harmony salt* - all-important in achieving the Great Work - by this name. Perhaps, as Serge Hutin confided to us, it is for that reason that the symbolic "sea-horse" was held in high esteem in the de Lesseps house. Was it considered to be an "ornamental" shield?

Our dearly departed friend thought that its presence on Montaigne Avenue undoubtedly meant that Pierre de Lesseps was himself Fulcanelli!

Could we not also imagine that, since the coat of arms should be read like a rebus (*uber*), then the tail of the hippocampus, which

---

[177] 'Blé' = 'dough' (Tr.).

seems to form the letter "J", might designate the initial of a first name (Jean, Jacques, Joël, ....?). Furthermore, as the "J" penetrates the heraldic *champagne*[178], it seems to "violate" it (phonetically: *violet*). In addition, as the *or*[179] terrace in base (*champagne d'or*) forms a letter "V", one could find there the first initial of the aforementioned word!

One last hypothesis: if one is aware that the totem or archaic emblem of the country of Armor - Armorica - was a hippocampus[180], might there possibly be a reference there to the Breton city of Hennebont, which was the city where Pierre Dujols' wife came from, and hence, perhaps Dujols would have been Fulcanelli? But in that case, why did he use the pseudonym *Magophon* (literally, the voice of Magus) for his *Hypotypose au Mutus Liber,* rather than *Fulcanelli*? Such incoherence is indeed difficult to explain!

However, a very powerful cabalistic element draws our attention, the more so as it brings us back again and again - thanks to the scholarly bookseller - to our previous hypothesis. The reader will recall that Eugène Canseliet always kept in mind that Jean-Julien Champagne was Pierre Dujols' close friend, and that Fulcanelli was also fond of Dujols, at least partly due to the fact that he was a descendent of the prestigious Valois family. As a matter of fact, the name *Valois* (qui vaut loi[181]) produces the anagram "*violas*": the Latin plural accusative of the noun, *viola*, which designates... the violet! This fact remains one that is decidedly impossible to overlook!

---

[178] Terrace in base: champagne in French, meaning the lower third in the coat of arms. (Tr.)

[179] Or = gold in heraldry. (Tr.)

[180] While the Dukes of Brittany had adopted the ermine in their coat of arms, in reference to Princess Hermione. It is also curious to note the presence of a shield with a hippocampus in the Hôtel de Ville in Paris. It was without a doubt already there in Fulcanelli's time.

[181] = that has the value of a law (Tr.).

# VIII
## Where the Master's Identity Finds the Light of Day

While Eugène Canseliet mentioned the name of Viollet-le-Duc no less than twelve times in his literary writings - never missing an opportunity to allude to the similarity between that name and the Master's surname - he likewise did not fail to allude to the *Feu du Soleil*[182] *("Vulcan-Helios")*, which designates the Master's nom de plume - Fulcanelli. The reader will also recall his reference to Raymond Roussel, the distinguished author of *Poussière de Soleils*[183]. and whom Jean-Julien Champagne had nicknamed "la classe". This is certainly not irrelevant!

Indeed, Eugène Canseliet wrote about that odd, hermetic interpretation given by the poet of the sealed star:

> Surprisingly gifted with alchemical perception, André Breton "mailed" to us, in the summer of 1948, the *vélin pur fil* copy of the *Cahiers de la Pléiade*[184], in which *"Fronton Virage"* provides a convincing overview of an unsuspected exegesis.[185]

In "Fronton Virage", André Breton indeed poses questions regarding a deep "secret" hidden by the one he considers "the greatest magnetiser of modern times", the works of whom are

---

[182] *The Sun's Fire.* (Tr.)
[183] *The Sun's Dust.* (Tr.)
[184] A well known edition of works of classic French authors. (Tr.)
[185] *Les deux Logis alchimiques*, éditions J.-J. Pauvert, 1979. Cf. our preface to Richard Danier's book, *L'Hermétisme alchimique chez André Breton*, éditions Ramuel.

interspersed with "cabalistic" processes drawing on the language of the birds that veils enigmatic truths. He wrote:

> Is it indeed conceivable that a man, *foreign to any initiatory tradition*, may consider himself bound to carry with him to the grave a secret of another order (that would after all be only his), *while supplying details that seem to be proof of a strong desire to see it unveiled*?

That "secret" was, of course – unless it was that of unlocking the Great Work, which we find dubious - that of the identity of Fulcanelli, with whom Raymond Roussel was perfectly acquainted since he had met him more than once at the de Lesseps town-house on Montaigne Avenue. The author of *La Doublure*[186] also occasionally met Jean-Julien Champagne there, whom, we will recall, he held in high esteem.

If references to the colour violet are numerous in the above-mentioned book by Raymond Roussel: "the golden lily on the violet flag" (pp. 122, 124, 125), it is, however, the title itself - *Poussière de Soleils* - that caught Eugène Canseliet's attention. Obviously, that expression was alluding to the sun's radiance. Did Eugène Canseliet thus refer to the scientific research carried out by the prominent scientist whose pseudonym "Fulcanelli" ("the Sun's fire") would have served to illustrate both his capacity as an alchemist, as well as his true identity?

Keeping in mind the idea that the Master's coat of arms, analyzed in the previous chapter, should be regarded as a rebus, one should note that a letter "J" (formed by the hippocampus' tail) can be seen penetrating, if not violating, the terrace in base (*champagne*) of the shield. Does not the latter also represent the letter "V"? Therefore, the initials of Fulcanelli's surname may well be J.V.(iollet?).

If one carefully reads the *Légende liminaire*[187] added by Eugène Canseliet, as well as the *Epilogue codicillaire*[188] in the manner of a will, to the last edition of *Deux Logis alchimiques* (1979) (which

---

[186] *The Understudy*. (Tr.)
[187] *Preliminary Legend*. (Tr.)
[188] *Codicillary Epilogue*. (Tr.)

preceded his disappearance by three years), one can see the famous Vessel of the Great Work painted by Jean-Julien Champagne in 1910. The clue is not without significance, when we read what Fulcanelli's disciple wrote in that respect:

> Assuredly, that work of art and thinking was the beneficiary of a positive miracle if one realizes that in 1940 it stayed under the eyes of looters who only ill-treated the woman blessed among all others - benedicta in mulieribus - in the pubis. The wound, although serious, healed perfectly under the hands of our dear friends Michel and Catherine Binda, master-surgeons for all damaged works of art, without them having left here and there a few other bruises inherent in the violation (*viol*), whatever it could be.

In that case, it was no doubt a "rape"("*viol*"), a fact that Eugène Canseliet had not failed to underline some eighteen years previously in his aforementioned article in the magazine, *La Tour Saint-Jacques*. The article was in fact *about the identity of the Adept Fulcanelli* to whom he had pledged not to commit "the double violation of the sworn secret and faith".

## "The Fire of the Sun" and Solar Radiation

This is how, very cunningly, Eugène Canseliet has led us from the *violet* to Viollet-le-Duc (*dux*: "I lead" in Latin), and from then to a certain J. "Viol", a prominent scientist!

Moreover, Robert Jolivet, the Abbé of Mont-Saint-Michel, refers to him cabalistically in this way:

J-O-L-I-V-E-T = J. VIOL EsT!

And such a character who answers every clue we have enunciated did indeed exist. He was the physicist, Jules Violle, born in 1841 in Langres in the Haute-Marne region, which adjoins the Champagne region[189]. Violle achieved his fame via his work on *solar radiation* and the establishment of *the unit of luminous intensity* which bears his name: the *Violle*. His research on the solar constant and atmospheric absorption led him to consider that the Sun's

---

[189] We will recall the "Master's shield" and its caption: "*uber campa agna*", in this instance designating the "fertile (soil) of Champagne" where he was born.

temperature was much lower than thought at the time, arguing that the higher the altitude, the less dense the atmosphere and lower the temperature. And this is precisely what Fulcanelli wrote in the following terms, in *Les Demeures philosophales*:

> High mountains remain crowned with snow despite the heat of the summer. In the elevated regions of the atmosphere, when the sun reaches the zenith, the cupolas of hot air balloons are covered with frost and their passengers suffer from intense cold. So, experience demonstrates that temperature goes down as altitude increases. Even light is only visible to us in as much as we are placed in its field of radiation. If we are outside the radiant beam, its action ceases for our eyes. It is a well-known fact that an observer looking at the sky from the bottom of a well at noon sees the starry night sky.
>
> Whence, then, do heat and light come from? From the simple shock of cold and dark vibrations against the gaseous molecules in our atmosphere. And since resistance increases in direct proportion to the density of the environment, heat and light are stronger on the surface of the earth than at great altitudes because the strata of air are also denser. Such is, at least, the physical explanation of the phenomenon. In fact, and according to hermetic theory, the opposition to the vibratory movement, the reactions are nothing more the first causes of an effect that translates into the liberation of luminous and fiery atoms from atmospheric air. Under the action of the vibratory bombardment, the spirit, freed from the body, takes on, for our senses physical qualities characteristic of its active phase: luminosity, radiance, heat.[190]

And to achieve his actinometrical studies on solar radiations, Jules Violle quite simply decided to go on a discovery tour to the top of Mont Blanc. He published the report, written in a light and pleasant style, in the *Revue des Deux Mondes*[191]. Here are a few excerpts that speak for themselves:

> However unavoidable that disturbing action (*that of the atmosphere*) may be, one can, by elevating oneself to a sufficient height, significantly attenuate it and, what is essential, attenuate it by a

---

[190] *Dwellings*, pp. 53-54.
[191] *The Two Worlds*. Founded in 1829 as a cultural, economic and political bridge between France and the United States of America. It is still active to this day. (Tr)

known ratio. The comparison between the measurements made at the base and at the top of the same mountain allows one to calculate the number to be found at the limit of the atmosphere, and the result will be even more accurate when the influence to be determined shows, on two levels, very different values - in other words, when the vertical distance between the two positions is more considerable. Consequently, what summit could be more fitting than Mont Blanc, the highest peak in Europe, to which, despite it's height, it was still nevertheless possible to carry a few physical instruments?

The expedition took place in mid-August of 1875. Jules Violle offers descriptions, not devoid of poetry, of the sumptuous landscapes he discovered then:

> The sun was rising when we reached the Dôme du Goûter. We were then happy to be allowed to contemplate one of the most beautiful and rare phenomena that can be witnessed in these high regions. In the atmosphere, opposite the Sun, Mont Blanc was casting a gigantic shadow, translucent enough to catch a glimpse behind it of the Tarentaise mountains. It was crowned in glory with rays of violet, one of which - of colossal proportions - was bending in the form of a plume of smoke toward Italy. The same apparition was observed in 1844, in the evening, by Messrs. Bravais, Martins and Lepileur, and in 1869 in the morning, by Mr Lortet, right about where we were standing.
>
> First of all, when I saw it, around 5:30 a.m., the shadow seemed to me higher than Mont Blanc itself. Its contours were so very sharp that we could easily distinguish the main curves of the mountain. Les Bosses du Dromadaire[192], in particular, were outlined with perfect neatness. That immense show is due, like the ones produced in theatres, to a reflection on a transparent mirror which, in this case, is the atmosphere itself. It lasted for more than one hour, decreasing in height as the Sun was rising above the horizon. The violet aura around the summit also disappeared little by little. The beam in the form of a plume of smoke in the direction of Italy remained visible longer, then also faded away. Those luminous appearances - the various phases of which we followed in this manner - can be easily explained. As a matter of fact, in the projection of Mont Blanc on the atmosphere, any gaseous column of a density other than the general mass of air must become visible on the air screen onto which it is

---

[192] The dromedary humps (Tr.).

projected, the difference in density necessarily resulting in a refrigerant power difference. Furthermore, this column exhibited a special colouring, similar to the first shades of dawn, which should also be attributed to the nature of the absorption exerted by the gas on the Sun's light.

[...] The sky is perfectly serene. The air absolutely calm. The thermometer in the shade indicates one degree above zero. Circumstances are therefore particularly favourable to the experiments I intend to carry out. Mr Margottet stands at his station, at the very foot of the Bossons glacier, 4,000 meters below me. Two series of simultaneous observations, one carried out at the summit, the other at the base of the mountain, shall provide the elements required for the accurate measurement of the quantity of heat sent by the Sun to the Earth, for the comparison of the two series will permit to assess, at any moment, the absorption due to the atmosphere.

One understands that careful assessment is indispensable. As a matter of fact, the amount of absorbed radiation depends not only on the thickness, but also on the physical condition, of the layer crossed at the moment considered. It is also very curious to note that, in this respect, on days when the air seems to us most limpid, when heavenly bodies shine particularly brightly, absorption is indeed greatest. It is now a well-established fact that some substances, perfectly transparent to light and to luminous heat, are in fact opaque to dark heat. Thus, the glass windows of a hot-house freely let through the whole portion of solar radiance that is simultaneously luminous and hot, but block the obscure caloric radiations issued from the soil or the plants. But our atmosphere always contains, and sometimes in significant quantities, a gas that is even less permeable to heat than glass; we mean water vapour. We are not talking here about visible vapour, condensed in the form of cloud or mist. We are talking about vapour that remains invisible, admirably transparent, and that is blended with air without altering its limpidity. Thanks to this substance, particularly abundant in the layers nearest to the ground, the atmosphere of the Earth is simultaneously a light garment able to temper summer heat, and a warm coat protecting it from the severe colds of winter; but the presence of that vapour represents a real difficulty as soon as one undertakes to assess solar heat.

[... ] The only means to solve the question consists in making measurements simultaneously at two positions located practically on the same vertical line that are on levels that are as far apart from each other as possible. This way, one can determine with all desirable accuracy the effect produced by an air column several kilometres high, while on the other hand the physical condition of that long gaseous column is accurately determined through the meteorological observations carefully made at each position. Such is the principle of the research I have been carrying out for more than two years, and in the prospect of which, before ascending Mont Blanc, I had already undertaken many ascents in the Dauphiné Alps.

The experimental process I have adopted is quite simple. The bulb of a mercury thermometer stands in the centre of a spherical vase and is kept at a temperature of zero degrees by means of ice piled up between that first vase, and a second one, external and concentric. A tubular aperture is made in this double-envelope system, which is oriented so that the solar rays fall freely on the bulb of the thermometer. The mercury immediately rises, and after about one hour it indicates a steady temperature that is used to measure the radiation intensity. Furthermore, one understands that the excess temperature shown on the thermometer in these circumstances permits one to assess the very temperature of the calorific source, i.e. the Sun.

[...] While taking into account the special circumstances - and in particular pressure - that may to some extent displace those very limits, one could not logically admit the billions of degrees that several physicists still recently thought possible to suggest for the temperature of the Sun. Last year, at the Allevard forge, I made comparative experiments on solar radiance and the radiation of a steel bath in full fusion at 1500 degrees, which completely confirmed the idea of a Sun only a few thousands degrees hot. The parallel between these experiments and others that I am carrying out, with the measurements made directly at the top of Mont Blanc, seems to lead even farther and to allow to numerically assess the real temperature at the Sun's surface.

One can easily see from the above lines that the expression "Fire of the Sun" cannot find a better match than with the French physicist, Jules Violle.

Let us briefly recall the life of the prominent scholar who satisfies, in every respect, the clues leading to the identity of Fulcanelli.

He was born in Langres on November 16, 1841, and, as a matter of fact, several references to Langres and its outskirts appear as if by chance in *Le Mystère des Cathédrales*!

The first gothic cathedral seen by Jules Violle was undoubtedly the one in Langres. Furthermore, on the date of his "communion privée[193]" in 1851, a *Cours d'archéologie sacrée*[194] was published, written by the Abbé Godard of the *Grand Séminaire*[195] in Langres, and approved by that diocese's bishop. This work seems not to have left the young boy indifferent, given his symbolic interests in sacred architecture. It includes a pertinent study of Egyptian monuments, and some very eloquent passages, such as the following:

> Certain traditions in our Masonic lodges link the body of masons of the Middle-Ages to Solomon and Hiram's troops of workers. The thread that links them is too tenuous, too ignored by History to be credible. However, who would refuse to recognize in the latter the type, in several respects, of God's image-carvers and lodgers' brotherhoods, such as the thirteenth century shows us, who were sometimes nomads and going where religion called them to erect basilicas, working without the help of beasts of burden and without making, at least in words, more noise than the shadows... [the analogy is obvious, cf. pp. 34-35 of this book.]

One sees flourish here the mind of the cathedral builders and those artists who remained anonymous, as Fulcanelli described. Furthermore, Fulcanelli alluded to the first emotions felt in his boyhood in the face of those gigantic masterpieces looming up from the Middle-Ages in *Le Mystère des Cathédrales* (pg. 35-36):

> The strongest impression of my early childhood - I was seven years old - an impression of which I still retain a vivid memory, was the emotion aroused in my young heart by the sight of a gothic cathedral. I was immediately enraptured by it. I was in ecstasy, struck with wonder, unable to tear myself away from the attraction of the marvellous, from the magic of such splendor, such immensity, such intoxication expressed by this more divine than human work.

---

[193] Religious ceremony where a Catholic child receives for the first time the holy communion, around the age of 7 (Tr.). First communion.
[194] *Course in Sacred Archeology.* (Tr.)
[195] Training college for the priesthood (Tr.). Seminary. (Tr.)

Since then, the vision has been transformed, but the original impression remains. And if custom has modified the spontaneous and moving character of my first contact, I have never acquired a defence against a sort of rapture when faced with those beautiful picture books erected on our parvises, and that raise to heaven their pages of sculptured stone.

In what language, through what means could we express to them our admiration, make witness to them of our thankfulness, all the feelings of gratitude that filled out heart, for all that they taught us to taste, to recognise, to discover, these masterpieces, these masters without word and voice.

It strikes us as very significant to discover that Jules Violle's grandfather, a surveyor in Dijon, authored a famous *Traité complet des carrés magiques*[196], the ancient vocation of which - according to the esoteric Tradition - dealt with pentagrams and talismans of all sorts. This influence in his early environment undoubtedly must have aroused a curiosity in the child and awakened in him a strong interest in mathematics, a subject his father was in fact teaching at Langres college, in succession of his other grandfather.

Born into such a family, and after brilliant secondary studies, the young Jules Violle could only envisage a scientific career. In 1861, he was simultaneously accepted at the *Ecole Polytechnique* and *Ecole Normale Supérieure*.[197] He opted for the latter, where he came out first at the entrance examination in physical sciences. In 1864, he was appointed professor at the *Lycée de Besançon* (Besançon High School), and the following year in Dijon, where he felt quite at home since his grandfather was living in Fixin. In 1867, Pasteur called him to the *Ecole Normale Supérieure* to become a natural-sciences laboratory assistant in Lacaze-Duthier's laboratory. As stated by Mr. A. Boutaric in his erudite biographical note about Violle, published under the auspices of the Dijon *Academy of Sciences, des Arts, et des Belles-Lettres*:

---

[196] *Comprehensive Treatise on Magical Squares* (Tr.).
[197] The two schools of higher education for those who would become the French elite. (Tr.)

In our time of out and out specialization, it seems surprising that a future physicist has inaugurated his scientific career with *anatomical or physiological* research. In reality, as he readily admitted, the patient dissections he carried out for one year constituted an excellent preparation to the delicate physical experiments he was to undertake later. His work is, indeed, entirely experimental and little of it is purely theoretical.

One year later, Jules Violle was appointed as an assistant in the physics laboratory of the same school, and busied himself working on his doctoral thesis on the subject of *"the mechanical equivalent of heat"*, which he was going to present at the Sorbonne in 1870. His testing equipment consisted of a metal disc rotating steadily between the poles of an electro-magnet. The heat resulting from the induced currents - the so-called Foucault currents - was measured in several metals (copper, zinc, lead, aluminium). Thus, as stated by Michel Atten in his study:

> [...] Already from the first steps, recorded in several articles, one can see the appearance of a practice of accurate measurement taking, which will be pursued throughout his whole life.

We shall indeed have many opportunities to observe this when studying the prominent savant's works.

Let us note here also that Violle was in Paris during the Commune uprising, and that he was mobilized by Marcellin Berthelot and Viollet-le-Duc, then a Lieutenant-Colonel, to defend the French capital, *as Eugène Canseliet affirmed about Fulcanelli.*

In 1872 Violle was appointed Professor of Physics at the Grenoble Faculty of Science. There he undertook a long series of tests on solar radiation and pertinent meteorological issues. To this end, we have already seen that he climbed Mont Blanc (in August 1875) in order to make actinometrical measurements using his ingenious "metallic-bulb thermometer". He also traveled to the Sahara desert to determine, under various atmospheric circumstances, the solar constant, i.e. the quantity of heat received at the limit of the terrestrial atmosphere by a normal surface with a 1 cm2 ray (*"Voyage scientifique en Algérie"*[198], in *Club Alpin*, 1877).

---

[198]*Scientific Trip in Algeria.* (Tr.)

Here is how he obtained the first solar-constant value that had a high probability of accuracy:

> To obtain a valid assessment of the Sun's temperature, says A. Boutaric, Mr Violle compared its radiance with that of sources that he carefully chose as exceptional: these were steel castings at the Allevard Forges, then molten-platinum baths. He showed that, contrary to what was then assumed, the average temperature at the solar surface does not go beyond a few thousand degrees. [...]
>
> Studying *solar radiation always was Violle's concern*. He insisted in particular on the importance of measurements taken from hot air balloons at very high altitudes. The readings achieved with Teisserine de Bord at heights reaching more than 15,000 meters (i.e. at the limit of atmosphere) represent important meteorological documents.

We will recall what Fulcanelli wrote on that subject (see above), and which precisely corroborates these statements:

> In the high regions of the atmosphere, when the heavenly body reaches the zenith, the cupola of hot air balloons is covered in ice and their passengers are exposed to very stiff cold.[199]

And we can't but give in to the temptation of adding to the above the following excerpt from *L'Autre Monde*[200], written by Savinien Cyrano de Bergerac and quoted by Eugène Canseliet in his second preface to *Les Demeures philosophales*:

> [...] One will not be surprised that I got nearer and nearer to the Sun without being burnt, for what burns is not fire, but the matter it is attached to, and the Sun's fire cannot be mixed with any matter.

In 1874 Jules Violle published his first Memorandum to the Academy of Sciences on "the Sun's temperature", followed two years later by his "Conclusions of actinometrical measurements at the top of Mont Blanc". He then adapted his ingenious actinometer to obtain absolute measurements by attaching it to a recorder, which consequently made it extremely useful to meteorological stations. In an attempt to address the concerns of farmers, he also dealt with issues related to lightning, ball lightning, and hail.

---

[199] *Les Demeures philosophales*.
[200] *The Other World*. (Tr.)

In 1877, he published a Memorandum on the average temperature of the surface of the sun. That same year he presented a report on the use of the radiometer as a demonstration apparatus. Interestingly, the radiometer came into existence thanks to the British physicist-chemist, William Crookes, who also had a passion for alchemy! It was in fact a kind of "solar windmill", or "light mill", that converted solar light into kinetic energy. Small wings, alternately white and black, are placed in equilibrium in a partially vacuumed flask. The warmer the molecules in the flask become, the higher the pressure becomes on black surfaces and, in consequence of Brown's theory, the wings begin turning in proportion to the solar radiance.

En 1878, he published "*Les Mesures actinométriques relevées en Algérie pendant l'été de 1877*"[201], following his expedition to the Sahara. That same year, he also published two essays on the specific temperature and melting point of palladium, and on the latent melting point of platinum, respectively. He also published an article on "solar heat" in the *Revue des Cours scientifiques*.

**Dumas, Berthelot, Lesseps and... "High Temperatures"**

Meanwhile, Violle's wife, Anna Jacob, had already presented him with two sons: Bernard and James, one year apart. Appointed Professor of Physics at the Lyons Science Faculty in 1879, he pursued his second research theme on high temperatures, which he started when he was in Grenoble. To this end, he decided to carry out a precise and accurate study of the melting points of rare metals such as palladium, iridium, and above all, platinum. Parallel to this, he developed a measuring method in one year using a glass balloon flask with a narrow neck and double walls, in between which he created a vacuum, thus permitting the very slow cooling of the liquid contained within, which was most effective when the inside of the double wall was silver-plated. It is, in a manner of speaking, the forerunner of the "thermos" bottle, the properties of which, clearly defined by Jules Violle, enabled d'Arsonval and Dewar to use similar containers for the preservation of liquefied gases.

---

[201] *Actinometrical Measurements Made in Algeria in the Summer of 1877.* (Tr.)

The same year, he published articles on the radiation of incandescent platinum, solar radiation measurements, specific temperatures and melting points of various refractory metals, and a "Report to the Rome Meteorological Convention on Question XIX: Measuring Solar Radiation, and the Role of Water Vapour Contained in the Atmosphere" (reprinting: Gauthier-Villars, Paris).

It is from the year 1879 on that Jules Violle, already very impressed by the erudition of the old scholar Eugène Chevreul, undertook a sustained correspondence with Jean-Baptiste Dumas to whom he had already submitted his previous memoranda, which he addressed at that time to *"Monsieur le Secrétaire Perpétuel*[202]*"* (of the Academy of Sciences). This time, his letters are preceded either by: *"Monsieur et Illustre Maître*[203]*"*, or *"Monsieur et Vénéré Maître*[204]*"*, as in the following letter, dated October 27 and written at the Hotel Corneille in Paris:

> Sir and Revered Master;
>
> I regret not meeting you. I had come to pay my respects to you while in Paris. I was also bringing you the enclosed short Note for the Academy. It is the continuation of my research on specific heats at high temperatures, research undertaken with the double objective of closely studying elevated temperatures accurately for the fifth time. I am providing here the melting points of gold and copper, not well known up to now, as well as the melting point of iridium, i.e. that is to say close to the temperature burning in oxygen.
>
> This last measurement was extremely difficult to carry out.
>
> Please accept, Sir and Revered Master, my very respectful and grateful regards.

In a letter sent from Lyons, dated April 19, 1880, J. Violle alludes to the friendly relations he and his wife, Anna, have with Jean-Baptiste Dumas and his family after making some appreciative remarks on Lyons Society of the time:

---

[202] Sir, the Permanent Secretary. (Tr.)
[203] Sir and Illustrious Master. (Tr.)
[204] Sir and Revered Master. (Tr.)

Sir and Illustrious Master,

I have taken to the Rhone Société d'Enseignement professionnel[205] the information you did me the honour of requesting from me. [...]

On its Board of Directors are found most commendable men, with quite varied political opinions. (Mr Vautier, Mr Mangini[206], etc.). However, it is undeniable that the mind that drives it is influenced by the city in which its headquarters are located, and it is frankly Republican and anti-clerical. The ceremony you are requested to chair will take place at the Grand-Théâtre in the presence of a considerable number of people, all of the shareholders (about one thousand of them), and many people who are foreign to the Society; an audience highly sympathetic to the Society and quite mixed, including the most recent chairmen, Messrs. Laborlaye, Tachero and Jules Simon. Last year, it was there that Mr Jules Simon, in a rather politically-tinted speech, commented on his conversion, which brought him closer to the right: loud comments the next day in the Lyons newspapers.

Yesterday, I had the honour of seeing Madam your grand-daughter, whose health appeared to me to be as satisfactory as possible. Mr Noël Dumas took advantage of the opportunity of some nice weather to take a long tour of Fourvières and neighbouring places with a friend.

Mrs. Violle, unfortunately still affected by Lyons' climate, joins me in sending her deepest respects to Mrs. Dumas. If vocational training does not succeed in attracting you to us, we still place our hopes in Royat where Madam, your grand-daughter, told me you intend to visit later this year. [...]

It is to be noted of Jules Simon, whom the above letter references, that he was a philosopher, a *spiritualist* and a politician. He was also Minister of Public Education in the National Defence government. It is as a moralist that Fulcanelli quotes him in his *Les Demeures philosophales*[207]:

> "In our century," said Jules Simon very appropriately, "one must walk or run: the one who stops is lost."

---

[205] Society for Vocational Training. (Tr.)
[206] The Senator's brother. (Tr.)
[207] *Dwellings*, p. 503.

According to the departed Jean Laplace, who possessed a photograph showing him in excellent company on Montaigne Avenue, was one of Ferdinand de Lesseps's usual guests, as were Jean-Baptiste Dumas and, of course, Jules Violle himself, which I was able to confirm with my own eyes.

In the following letter, dated September 3, 1881, Jules Violle informs Jean-Baptiste Dumas of his renewed wish to be allowed to practice in the capital city, in view of his competency and his wife's health:

> Thus, I will not be bold enough, Illustrious Master, to commend myself to the indulgent benevolence you deign impart on me. However, I owe that benevolence an explanation of the reasons that brought about my application.
>
> The first reason is health-related: the moist climate in Lyons is very bad for Mrs. Violle. The second reason, dear Master - which I'm not afraid to tell you - is a deep distaste for my current position after the promises made to me upon entering the Ecole Normale, whereas after being accepted at the Ecole Polytechnique and the Ecole Normale, I was pressed to join the latter, after a successful examination that Mr Pasteur was kind enough to consider brilliant, after 20 years of service and work that I am not entitled to judge, I am here a third-class professor at the level of the most recent deputy-lecturer, nominated titular professor six months ago. It is true that I have here collections in ruins, a laboratory that you know, and no money. To compensate for all this, I have the certainty that when there is a vacant position in physics in Paris, I will see anybody, and perhaps not even a physicist, preferred to me. But I have said too much. Please excuse me, dear and illustrious Master, and, if at all possible, deign to help me...

In the next letter, dated September 9, 1881, Jules Violle refers to the previous one and alludes to his friend, Marcellin Berthelot:

> So, I dare beseech you not to show my previous letter to anyone - not even to Mr Berthelot - even though I have always viewed him as someone benevolent and well-disposed toward me. However, he has the sorrows of authority and the responsibility not to empty the province [...]
>
> I shall not reiterate the reasons for my strong desire to go back to

Paris. Your powerful influence alone can bring me back there and help me overcome this critical point in my career...

Let us add for the record that Jean-Baptiste Dumas was indeed a very well-known personality at that time. More than just the permanent secretary of the Academy of Sciences - which was already a great deal in itself - he had also been admitted to the *Académie française* in 1876, and was fully at home in the political world since he had been, in turn, Minister of Agriculture, Senator, and Deputy[208]. Further, he had associated with Ferdinand de Lesseps and had been fervently welcomed at the town-house on Montaigne Avenue more than once.

In 1878, he chaired the International Metric Commission and managed to get the principle of the French meter and kilogramme accepted by 19 out of 20 states. In 1881, he chaired the International Monetary Conference and the Convention of Electricians in Paris, which Jules Violle himself had actually participated in as well.

**From High Temperatures to "Thermo-Master"**

Pursuing his work on palladium and platinum's high melting temperatures, Jules Violle managed to overcome the difficulties by using quite remarkable means: it was with electrical arcs consuming more than 100 HP that he measured the temperature of the positive crater and hence could assess that, even higher, of the flame springing up from that crater.

The International Convention of Electricians had asked the question and had raised the issue of the impossibility of defining the source of light constituted by flames. Jules Violle, who had been struck during the course of his experiments by "the beauty and fixity of the light issuing from a bath of liquid platinum" (his own terms), proposed to the assembly the audacious idea of setting up a new "light standard", using the surface unit of molten platinum at his solidification temperature as the basis. His proposal, while ingenious, was too innovative and did not obtain a consensus. It was, however, held for the future, and Jean-Baptiste Dumas approved it

---

[208] Member of Parliament (Tr.). MP.

without reservation. From then on, Jules Violle oriented his research in that direction and established a variety of *temperature measurements* around that of melting platinum, at 1,775°C.

And here, although it may seem out of place at first glance, is where we should recall *Les Voyages en Kaléidoscope*, by Irène Hillel-Erlanger, as well as her famous *thermometer* designed by the well-known painter, Van Dongen. If one recalls that the book not only veiled the process of the Great Alchemical Work, but also the personality of a certain ... adept, one will then better understand the reference since the thermometer then becomes, thanks to the language of the birds, the *"thermo-master"*! Fulcanelli, indeed!

> [...] A Standard-Thermometer presides over our salutory destinies. [...] The THERMO-MASTER guards us against ourselves: Ideal revealer. Centre of gravity. Incomparable Precision and Decision Instrument....

The whole book is in the *Dada* surrealist style, which somehow evokes the sea-horse, the hippocampus, or else the sire horse, the stallion (*"etalon"* in French) (from lower Latin *Stalto, -onis*), also phonetically designating a "unit of measurement"[209]!

## The Light Standard and Accumulated Evidence

Let's go back to the year 1878, when the master of Jules Violle presided over the International Metric Commission that succeeded in getting the meter accepted as the unit of measurement. We discover that Fulcanelli writes about this very thing in his *Les Demeures philosophales*?

> The X [Greek Khi] is the emblem of measure (μετρον i.e. metron) taken in all its meanings: dimension, area, space, duration, rule, law, boundary or limit. For this *occult* reason, the *international standard of the meter,* made of platino-iridium and kept at the pavilion of Breteuil in Sèvres, has the shape of an X in its profile. All bodies of nature, all beings either in their structure or their appearance, abide by this fundamental law of radiation, all are subjected to this *measure*.[210]

---

[209] *L'étalon* has the meaning in French of being a unit of measure. (Tr.)
[210] *Dwellings*, p. 199.

And in a footnote, at the bottom of the same page, Fulcanelli writes:

> We are not speaking here of copy no.8, registered with the *Conservatoire des Arts et Métiers* in Paris that is used as a legal standard, but about the international prototype.[211]

The Adept was well informed, and this for the very excellent reason that he had worked on the project at the International Bureau of Weights and Measures at the Breteuil Pavilion. He had obviously wished to imprint the "X" occult sign into the metric standard and thereby immortalise it. We should keep in mind that some time earlier he wrote the following few lines:

> The Greek X and the French X represent *the writing of light through light itself*, the trace of its passing, the manifestation of its movement, the affirmation of its reality. It is its true signature.[212]

Following that is a veritable panegyric to the X in which he states that it is the complete number of the Great Work since the unity, the two natures, the three principles and the four elements merge as the double quintessence, the two Vs – two fives - joined in the Roman digit "X", i.e. the number ten. The basis of *Pythagoras' Cabala* can be found in this numeral, or the basis of the universal language, an odd paradigm of which can be seen on the last leaf of a little book on alchemy entitled, *La Clavicule de la Science Hermétique*[213], written by "a denizen of the North during his leisure time", 1732, Amsterdam.

Indeed, if one goes to the leaf in question, here is what can be read:

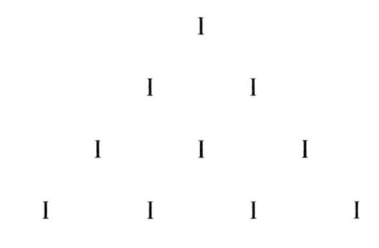

```
              I

           I     I

        I     I     I

     I     I     I     I
```

---

[211] Ibid.
[212] Ibid. p. 198.
[213] *The Clavicule of Hermetic Science*. (Tr.)

These units together give the number X, perfect, which, anatomically dissected through the middle, the left horn being erected perpendicularly, results in the letter L, but the two horns being put together give the letter V and, as a whole, the letter X, resulting in LVX, (light) which is only one word through which it pleased God to leave to man some idea about Him.

Perhaps just a mere coincidence, or perhaps an additional clue, who knows? The coat of arms of the City of Langres, where Jules Violle was born, in fact bears a Saint-Andrew's cross - X - on *fleurs-de-lis-adorned field of azure.*

Later, an eminent colleague, P. Villard, said about him:

> The great questions that come first in general physics retained Mr Violle's attention, and particularly the capital problem of the radiance of bodies at high temperatures. A long series of research works, broadly dealt with, were carried out by him to study solar radiation, to measure elevated temperatures, to create light-standards...

To which we might add the following excerpt from the rather strange *Voyages en Kaleidoscope,* by I. Hillel-Erlanger:

> Soon, he had mastered the fluidic forces that rule the World. And the secret of which is not completely buried since the Very-Sublime-Antiquity. Docile to his commands, these forces merge with their captive brothers; Rays; Radiating Bodies....

A previous passage is also very compelling when considering our conclusion that the subject was Fulcanelli:

> Joël Joze reviews his *volcanic* past. Fire outflow, cooled lava. Adolescence hypnotised by Positive Sciences. Physics, Chemistry, Photogenic research mainly. [...] Already, however, some surprising discoveries; Praised to the skies by the vanguard; disparaged by querulous conservatives...

As a matter of fact, Jules Violle based his research primarily on light and its radiance, luminescence; that of the sun to start with, later, that of molten metals such as palladium, platinum, silver, and zinc, until setting up a photometric standard for acetylene in 1896. In 1881, he published an article entitled, *Intensités lumineuses des radiations émises par le platine incandescent*[214], as well as an overall report on the law of radiation.

*The Calorimeter developed by physicist Jules Violle*

Our prominent physicist steadily pursued his research work throughout the year of 1882, sending Jean-Baptiste Dumas endless requests to be transferred to the capital city. In the meantime, his household was expanding as yet another two children were born: Louis in 1881, and Henri in 1882. That same year, he sent J. B. Dumas a rather terse letter, dated April 2:

> Sir and Illustrious Master,
>
> Everything considered, I prefer to say nothing in response. It is not possible for me to tell the whole truth; I prefer to keep silent. Therefore, I beg you to accept to suppress my reply.
>
> Please accept …..[…]

---

[214] *Luminous Intensities of the Radiations Emitted by Incandescent Platinum* (Tr.).

What could that be about? Perhaps it had something to do with the question raised in a previous letter, dated March 10, which read as follows (unless it was about a secret carefully kept since then):

> I take the liberty of attaching to this letter a short summary of my most important works. I also attach a Note on the boiling temperature of zinc. In the past, this question has given rise to such a lively discussion between Mr Deville and Mr E. Becquerel that, although certain that I am in the right, I hardly dare send it to you, and pray you to keep it to yourself if you think it may be prejudicial to anyone.

That controversy was again alluded to in the next letter, dated March 31, in which the unceasing integrity and modesty that do credit to our prominent physicist, corroborate the preceding statement:

> Which does not prevent Mr Troost from stating that it was a number published long ago, which he only obtained through faulty calculations. The worst in all of that is that being quite committed as far as Mr Deville is concerned, and preferring a thousand times to lose the result of a work rather than affecting his glory in any way, I may not say what I thus dare confide to you....

On September 22 of the same year, the following letter reached J. B. Dumas:

> I am impatient, indeed, to start this work on the light standard. Already one month has passed, and no time is to be lost to get to the desired epoch. There certainly will be practical difficulties, and the genuine solution will not be found without trouble. Consequently, I beg you to insist so that my situation can be wound up and I can come and work with you as soon as possible.

The next year, in 1883, thanks to Jean-Baptiste Dumas's mediation in his favour, Jules Violle finally received a 5,000 franc grant from the Ministry of Post and Telegraph in order to enable him to pursue his research on the light standard. A similar amount of money was also decided in his favour by the Ministry of Trade, but he waited for it in vain.

During that year, Jules Violle travelled frequently to Paris, were he resided at 15 rue de l'Estrapade, near the Panthéon. It is from there that he addressed the following letter, dated October 31, to J. B. Dumas:

> I am not neglecting the standard for light. I already have a fairly practical means to indefinitely maintain the platinum close to its melting temperature. I hope to be requested soon to deliver a lecture at Ecole Normale, and then be able to complete the research relating to the quality of the light emitted under various incidences by silver and platinum at their melting temperatures at the physics laboratory ....

And in the letter below, dated December 1 of the same year, Jules Violle expresses his dearest wishes:

> What is still lacking, alas, is a laboratory. However, it would be very easy to provide me with one. It would be enough to appoint me as a lecturer at Ecole Normale. Mr Dumort and Mr Berthelot fully agree on the usefulness of such a thing. [...]

> It is cruel to be deprived of a laboratory that would currently be so useful. I do not mention a salary, for it could be but very modest. However, simply lecturing at L'Ecole would not prevent me from teaching elsewhere. The other day, I actually met Mr Jamin who told me in confidence that creating positions for new lecturers at the Sorbonne was being considered, and that he would be pleased to see me on their lists....

After having published an article on the boiling temperature of zinc the year before, he wrote an article, published in 1883, on the radiation of solidifying silver. In this respect, we will recall Blaise de Vigenère's *Particulier* (*Traité du Feu et du Sel*[215]), which had deeply interested both Fulcanelli and his disciple, Eugène Canseliet, for the whole problem of superfusion (be it of lead or silver) is emphasized there. Obviously, our scholar was mastering its process perfectly.

Jules Violle continued commuting between Lyons and Paris until the next year (1884) when he finally obtained his appointment as a lecturer at *Ecole Normale Supérieure*.

Augustin Boutaric explains the circumstances in which our ingenious physicist finally managed to define the unit of light intensity:

---

[215] *Particulier Treatise on Fire and Salt* (Tr.).

Violle had suggested taking one square centimetre of platinum at its melting point. This proposal having been accepted, he undertook a long series of research works that set up the constancy of the new standard and the ratio between its intensity and that of the "Carcel" lamp that was used before as the photometric unit (one carcel is 481/1000 of the new standard). By its constancy, no less than by its whiteness and its intrinsic brightness, which is about *eleven* times that of the carcel, platinum at its melting temperature meets all the requisites that can be expected from a prototype standard, which must represent an invariable comparison term for ordinary standards. The name of Violle will forever remain attached to the new light unit.

Liquid silver at solidifying temperature offers, in conditions easy to achieve, an incandescent surface of perfect neatness and in a rigorously determined state. Violle used it to study various questions pertaining to the emission phenomenon: variations in radiation intensity with incidence: polarisation of the emitted light, etc.

There was great interest in the choice of such a light source, and the International conference then unanimously adopted the new "light standard" (equivalent to twenty decimal candle-power units) to which the name of Jules Violle has remained attached ever since, as it owed to him its official designation: the Violle standard.

*Physicist Jules Violle in his garb as member
of the Academy of Sciences*

# IX
# The Parisian Career of the Savant

In the same year (1884) that he achieved his fame, Jules Violle published a Memorandum to the Academy of Sciences on *"l'étalon absolu de lumière"*[216] (C.R., t.98), as well as a book containing the sum of his works on that subject: *Expériences faites en vue de déterminer l'unité absolue de lumière*[217] (Editions Gauthier-Villars). Parallel to that, the first volume of his *Cours de Physique*[218], dedicated to molecular physics, was seeing the light [the second one was in three parts: acoustics (1888), geometrical optics (1892), and physical optics (1892)].

On April 11 of that year, his "dear and illustrious Master", Jean-Baptiste Dumas, passed away - the very one who had always been so considerate to him, whose friendship had been unfailing, and who had entrusted to him as a last task, the checking of "kilogram standards" for which Jules Violle had already made preliminary measurements at Sèvres, in the Breteuil Pavilion for Weights and Measures. Decidedly, work with high-precision measurements seemed to naturally devolve to him.

So it was that our eminent physicist was also led to show interest in determining the speed of sound wave propagation. Although numerous measurements had been taken in the nineteenth century, the results obtained were not satisfying as they left room for a margin of uncertainty, i.e. between 330.6 and 332.3 meters per second.

---

[216] Absolute light-standard (Tr.).
[217] *Experiments Carried Out with a View to Determining the Absolute Light Unit* (Tr.).
[218] *A Course in Physics* (Tr.).

In 1885, Jules Violle, in collaboration with Vautier, implemented a wide-span device: a 70 cm-diameter U-shaped pipe, some 13 kilometres long. Finding inspiration in the detection apparati developed by Regnault, and then by Marey, he found a slightly higher speed - 331meters per second - and determined the shape of the acoustic wave, as well as the way in which it evolves during the propagation. He went back to these experiments in 1888, then again in 1895 at Argenteuil, this time with a shorter pipe, but a wider diameter (3 meters). This enabled him to confirm the results obtained and to accurately determine the range of sound, which depends on frequency.

In 1888, Violle was presented with a fifth son, Gabriel, and successfully completed the *"Comparaison des énergies totales émises par le platine et l'argent fondants*[219]*"* (C.R. Ac. Sc.t.7).

### Les Arts et Métiers

In 1897, after the death of E. Becquerel, the Improvement Council of the *Conservatoire National des Arts et Métiers* decided, on Mr Mascart's urging, to elect our provincial physicist as a professor: "Violle is an initiator!" exclaimed the latter, in the midst of the debates. The appointment became effective in December.

Despite the decrepitude of the laboratory equipment that went with the CNAM physics professorship, Jules Violle expressed his enthusiasm for having been accepted in the capital city by fully dedicating himself to his lectures, which were given on mechanics (gravity and elasticity), acoustics, optics, electricity, and magnetism.

The Vertbois fountain in the yard at the entrance of the Conservatoire National des Arts et Métiers, which showed a very symbolic low-relief, obviously had not escaped the eye of the scientist who was now well into his 50s. We note that Fulcanelli dedicated no less than ten pages in his *Les Demeures philosophales* to the copious description of this motif:

---

[219] *Comparison of the Total Energies Emitted by Melting Platinum and Silver* (Tr).

*Jules Violle teaching his course at Art et Métiers*

Built in 1633 by Benedictine monks of Saint-Martin-des-Champs, this fountain was originally erected inside the priory leaning against the surrounding wall. In 1712, the monks offered it to the City of Paris, for public use, along with the grounds needed to rebuild it, provided "that the site would be established in one of their convent's old towers and that an outer door would be placed there". The fountain was thus placed against the so-called Tower of Vertbois, located on rue Saint-Martin and took the name of Saint-Martin's fontaine which it kept for more than a century.

The small structure, restored at the expense of the government in 1832, is made up of "a shallow, rectangular niche flanked by two Doric pilasters, with vermiculated embossments, which support an architravated cornice. On the cornice is built a kind of small helmut crowned by a winged cartouche. A sea conch tops the cartouche. The upper part of the niche is occupied by a frame in the centre of which a vessel is sculpted." [220]

---

[220] *Dwellings*, pp. 309-310.

In fact, many who do not pay great attention to detail see in this subject the heraldic Ship of the City of Paris, without considering that it offers to the curious mind an enigma of an entirely different truth *and of a less mundane order.*

> Surely the relevance of our observation may be questioned and, where we recognize an enormous stone attached to the edifice of which it forms an integral part, some may see only an ordinary parcel of goods. But in this case, one would be quite embarrassed to find a reason for the set sail, not completely brailed up on the yard of the main mast, a peculiarity that highlights the sole and bulky parcel, thus purposely unveiled. The purpose of the creator of the sculpture is therefore obvious: it is about an occult load, normally safe from prying eyes, and not about a parcel travelling on a deck.[…]
>
> It is the most delicate part of the work, that when the prime coagulation of the stone, unctuous and light, appears at the surface and floats on waters. […]
>
> So, to show evidence that the Fontaine du Vertbois was originally dedicated to philosophal water, the mother of all metals and basis of the Sacred Art, the Benedictine monks of Saint-Martin-des-Champs had sculpted, in the cornice supporting the low-relief, various attributes related to this fundamental liquor. Two crossed oars and a caduceus support Hermes's petasus, represented under the modern aspect of a winged armet[221] on which a little dog is watching. A few ropes issuing from the visor uncoil onto the oars and the God of the Work's winged staff.[222]

Indeed, it is the most delicate phase of the Great Work that is referred to by our Adept, since it is about the "reincrudation" of the elected metal, consisting in making it "raw": the famous *sublimations*[223] that release the cubic stone or "ice cube", the celebrated *rémore,* the obtaining process of which forever separates Alchemy from common chemistry. As Fulcanelli stated it in another text:

---

[221] Helmet (Tr).

[222] *Les Demeures philosophales.*

[223] cf. Our book *Alchimie: Science et Mystique* [translation - *Alchemy: Science and Mysticism*].

...of an odd device, which constitutes the *secretum secretorum* that was never revealed and probably never will be.[224]

And a little farther on:

Before proceeding, let us say about that unknown expedient - that from the chemical point of view should be considered absurd, preposterous or paradoxical - that it marks the crossing where alchemical science splits from chemical science. Applied to other bodies, it results, in the same circumstances, in as many unforeseen results, in substances with surprising properties. Hence, this unique and powerful means allows a development with an unsuspected scope, through the multiple new simple elements and the compounds derived from the said elements, but the genesis of which remains an enigma to the chemical reasoning. This, of course, should not be taught. If we have entered that preserved region of hermetics; if, bolder than our predecessors we have mentioned it, it is because we wished to show that: 1° alchemy is a genuine science – likely, as is chemistry, to spread and progress – and not the empirical acquisition of a precious metals trade secret; 2° alchemy and chemistry are both positive sciences, accurate and genuine, although different, in practice as well as in theory; 3° chemistry could not, for the above reasons, vindicate an alchemical origin; 4° finally, the innumerable properties, more or less wonderful, outright attributed by some philosophers to the sole philosopher's stone, each belong to the unknown substances obtained from chemical materials and elements, but processed following the secret technique of our Magisterium.[225]

This, at least, has the merit of being clear!

In 1892, Jules Violle published *"Sur le rayonnement des corps incandescents et la mesure optique des hautes températures"*[226], *"Sur le rayonnement des corps incandescents"*[227], and *"Sur la température de l'arc électrique"*[228].

---

[224] *Les Demeures philosophales*, t. I, p. 383.
[225] Ibid.
[226] *On the Radiation of Incandescent Bodies and High-Temperature Optical Measurement* (Tr).
[227] *On the Radiation of Incandescent Bodies* (Tr).
[228] *On the Temperature of the Electrical Arc* (Tr).

In 1893, our savant settled with his family - his wife and five children, among whom were two infants - at 89 boulevard Saint-Michel, opposite the Jardin du Luxembourg, very close to 47 rue Denfert-Rochereau (now rue Henri Barbusse) where Pierre Dujols and his wife stayed for many years.

During that year, Violle continued working on "*Le rayonnement des corps incandescents et la mesure des hautes temperatures*" (C.R., t. 114). The year after, in collaboration with Moissan, he worked on the development of an electric furnace and presented a memorandum on the "*Rayonnement des différents corps réfractaires chauffés dans un four électrique*[229]". Consisting of two carbon rods placed in a lime environment, which are bridged by an electric arc, the electric furnace later enabled Moissan to found the chemistry of high temperatures, all-important in metallurgy.

That same year, Jules Violle travelled to America to the Chicago Science Exhibition at the Chicago World Fair. Upon his return, he published "*Sur le point de fusion de l'or*"[230] in the *Revue générale des Sciences*[231] (t. V, 1894), as well as a study on the scientific movement in the United States and the Chicago exhibition in the *Revue des Deux-Mondes*.

In 1895, he published "*Le point de fusion de l'or*"[232](*La Nature*) and reported the connections between "*chaleur spécifique et point d'ébullition du carbone*"[233] (J.P., 3°S, t.6) because, as emphasized by A. Boutaric, he was naturally led in the course of his work on the "electric furnace" to study the functioning of the electric arc. He then showed that the glow of positive carbon rods does not depend on the intensity of the current that goes through the arc. According to him, the invariability of the glow, which indicates a constant temperature, corresponds with a well-determined physical phenomenon: carbon ebullition. Developing and perfecting the methods he had already offered for the determination of elevated

---

[229] *Radiance of Various Refractory Bodies Heated in an Electric Furnace* (Tr.).
[230] *On the Melting Point of Gold* (Tr.).
[231] *General Review of the Sciences*. (Tr.)
[232] *The Melting Point of Gold* (Tr.).
[233] *Specific heat and boiling point of carbon* (Tr.).

temperatures, he established the temperature of the positive crater at 3600°C, and that of the arc would likely take higher values, depending on the intensity of the electrical power.

Then, returning to his experiments with Vautier on sound propagation in a cylindrical pipe, he published those results that same year. He also proposed a new photometric standard based upon an acetylene lamp. As a matter fact, the incandescence potential of this gas is twenty times higher than that of coal gas burning in a Bengel burner, and at least six times higher than the same gas burning in an Auer burner. *"The acetylene flame has an actinic intensity that will be precious in the domain of photography"*; such was the conclusion in *Revue des Académies et Sociétés Savantes*[234] (13-1-1896). The latter reported that during its session held on 7 February of that year:

> Mr Violle indicates how he was able to obtain photographs by exciting fluorescence in an incandescence bulb by using *Tesla* current; the cathode circles the base of the lamp, the anode is a tin-foil strip stuck on the ampul's equator.

All those discoveries and multiple works - of which the list given here is by no means exhaustive - crowned the savant's work with success by finally opening the doors of formal recognition to him. In fact, in 1897, he was elected to the French Academy of Sciences, where he succeeded the great physicist, Fizeau. Two years later in England, he was appointed Member of the Royal Institution of Great Britain. It was on that occasion that Fulcanelli went to Edinburgh, Scotland to discover the fabulous sundial of Holyrood Palace. Again and again we find that every clue connects.

Jules Violle also had among his friends the great astronomer, Camille Flammarion, whom Fulcanelli mentions in *Le Mystère des Cathédrales* in reference to black virgins:

> Camille Flammarion tells us of a similar statue which he saw in the vaults of the Observatory on 24 September 1871, two centuries after the first thermometric observation made there in 1671.[235]

---

[234] *Review of the Academies and Learned Societies..* (Tr.)
[235] *Mysteries*, p. 60.

On June 3, 1903, the savant mourned the loss of his son, Bertrand, who died on the family property in Fixin.

In 1907, Jules Violle became a member of the *Commission d'Examen des Inventions intéressant l'Armée de Terre et de Mer*[236] (which he chaired in 1911). During the course of 1908, he presented memoranda on hail storms, and on the action of lines, as well as a "*Rapport sur la nécessité de l'application exacte du système métrique decimal à toutes nos monnaies*"[237] (16 March 1908), addressed to Mr. Mazerolle. His works on agricultural meteorology resulted in him becoming a member of the *Académie d'Agriculture* the following year.

Incidentally, we would like to tell an anecdote that deserves mentioning. In the autumn of 1911, Jules Violle submitted a memorandum entitled, "*Sur un Retour momentané des Fleurs doubles d'un Rosier à la Forme simple*"[238] to the Academy of Sciences:

> During that vacation period I had an opportunity to observe a fact that to me seems to deserve mentioning. This fact was presented to me by a magnificent "Gloire de Dijon" rosebush planted in the ground some ten years ago at Fixin that has shown a remarkable development and vigour. [...]
>
> Then, suddenly, around September 12, it produced a full florescence of absolutely single roses on all its branches, to which, eight days later, a full blooming of the customary beautiful roses replaced them on all those very same branches,which went on as usual and which were still adorning the rosebush when I left the country several days ago. (C.R., 1911, t.153).

It should be added that the savant used to carry out particular experiments in his garden, across which he stretched copper wires, thus obtaining astonishing results in the breeding of cultivated plants!

---

[236] *Commission for the Examination of Inventions of Interest to Land and Air Forces* (Tr).
[237] *Report on the Necessity to Accurately Apply the Decimal Metric System to All Our Currencies* (Tr).
[238] *On a Temporary Return from Double Flowers on a Rosebush to the Single Form* (Tr).

That year saw the triumph of the wireless telegraph and the wireless radio; discoveries made possible thanks to his long-standing friend, Edouard Branly, who was deeply interested in mysticism and was a fervent Christian, like himself. In passing, let us say that Edouard Branly was also working on the temperatures of the Sun. From the age of 22, he was an assistant to the physicist, Paul Dessains, who submitted to the Academy of Sciences a first Note by his young assistant in 1869: a study on solar radiation at various altitudes, made on the Righi Mountain in Lucerne (Switzerland). This study, which allowed the determination of solar radiation absorption by water vapour, truly gave a boost to modern meteorology. These concerns were something that he held in common with his good friend, Jules Violle.

With the out-break of war in 1914 - a year that saw the death of his youngest son, Gabriel, fallen on the field of battle - Jules Violle then decided to put his knowledge to use in the service of his country. The following year, he was appointed President of the High Commission for Inventions in the Interest of National Defence. He gave lectures at the CNAM on the role of physics during the war, as well as on the future of physical industries after the war. However, he deplored that the war was upsetting his idea of progress, which, in his opinion, *should be understood in the sense of a mellowing of manners, which would necessarily result in a bringing together of the prominent men of all nations.*

This indeed did not prevent him from analyzing, in a patriotic impulse, the various applications of science to the development of modern weapons with a view to emphasizing France's role in the forefront.

In the same way - as did his first master, Pasteur - he also insisted on the need for scientific research for his country:

> May the leaders of our largest manufactures be penetrated by these thoughts. Without research laboratories, no inventions, no improvement....

He deplored that a *Laboratoire Central des Poids et Mesures*[239] - an idea in which he had invested much of himself - had not been created. Here is how the great physicist, Ch. Ed. Guillaume, then Director of the International Office for Weights and Measures, referred to this eminent senior:

> In the first months of my stay in France, I had the privilege of a more direct contact with Mr J. Violle. In the winter, we used to take the train together when night had fallen, to arrive at dawn at the Breteuil pavilion where he was working on the programme of the French section. His simplicity, his kindness, his immense knowledge had a thorough effect on me. The first volume of his Course in Physics had just been published. I was reading it and we were discussing it... His love for science was absolutely unselfish and he was of a rare modesty, even among savants; he welcomed young physicists with benevolence, and gave them advice and encouragement. May it be permitted to one of those who had the privilege to approach him to express a recollection full of emotion and gratitude.

And it is precisely that same Ch.-Ed. Guillaume whom Fulcanelli emphatically recalled in his *Demeures philosophales* on the subject of the existence of *metallic life*:

> This metallic will, the very soul of metal, is clearly put forward in one of the most beautiful experiments carried out by Mr Ch.-Ed. Guillaume. A calibrated steel rod is submitted to a steady and progressive traction, the strength of which is recorded by means of a dynamograph. When the rod is about to break, it shows a narrowing that can be located accurately. The stretching action is then stopped and the rod is given again its original dimensions, then the test is restarted. This time, the narrowing takes place in a different place. When pursuing with the same technique it is noticed that all the points have successively been affected by giving in to the same traction. But if the steel rod is calibrated one last time, taking again the experiment from the beginning, it is observed that a much higher strength than the one at the start is needed to produce again the breaking symptoms. Mr Ch.-Ed. Guillaume concluded very wisely from these tests that the metal behaved like an organic body; it successively reinforced all its weak parts and purposely increased its coherence in order to better defend its threatened integrity.

---

[239] Central Laboratory for Weights and Measures (Tr.).

At this point of our study the reader will most assuredly not be surprised by such a reflection and its eminently alchemical significance.

Our learned man,[240] Violle, *officially* disappeared from his little village of Fixin on September 12, 1923, aged 83.

Augustin Boutaric wrote in his laudatory note:

> He was a great savant and a man of heart. His simplicity and his rectitude drew upon him nothing but sympathy.

But even here we discover a great curiosity.The death certificate was delivered by Henri Violle, one of Jules' sons who was a physician. This was certainly most unconventional, even highly questionable and not in accordance with legal conventions. Henri Violle is the son who shares his father's grave – along with his wife, born Suzanne Champy - while Jules Violle's own wife, Anna Jacob, had been buried the year before Violle's death in a neighbouring burial vault. All this is quite singular and gives much food for thought....

It is also interesting to note that Dr Henri Violle, a pharmacist, Doctor of Medicine, Doctor of Natural Sciences and elected member of the *Académie de Médecine*, had a brilliant career in epidemiology and bacteriology. While not wishing to dwell too long on the significance of his works, it is still troubling to observe that he had a passion for "metallic colloids" when one knows that *potable gold*,

---

[240] For all those who remain in doubt about Fulcanelli's true identity as proposed here, they should be informed that in the course of the author's long research sessions at the Institut, I discovered, slipped in among the carefully filed letters of Jules Violle, an old, flimsy sheet of paper on which the year 1927 was typed, as was the short accompanying text. In summary, it stated that the printer-publisher De Closet was informed, in that very year 1927, of Fulcanelli's real surname, which Violle! I certify the truth of this fact, as well as the authenticity of this additional evidence to be included in the file, although it was brought about quite fortuitously. I then deemed it appropriate to take it surreptitiously from among the precious documents, in order to be able to date it approximately with the help of an analysis of the paper and, above all, of the typing. Upon completion of these analyses, everything was in perfect match with the year 1927. Since then, I have felt unable either to discretely return this note to the file at the Institute, or to destroy it. It is still in my possession.

directly issuing from the philosopher's stone, in fact constitutes a type of "metallic colloid"!

In an article entitled *"Les Colloïdes thérapeutiques et l'anaphylaxie*[241]*"*, he wrote on this subject:

> The substances that play the part of antigens when inoculated into animals are considered as being of a colloidal nature. They alone seem to be able to trigger, in the body that has received them, the formation of antibodies....
>
> [...] Some physicians consider the strong reactive phenomena occurring when injecting mineral substances in "colloidal solutions" such as platinum, gold and silver salts as being of anaphylactic origin ....

It is at least odd to observe how much those concerns are close to those of Alchemy, where the Noble Matter, originally very toxic, has released its quintessence and permits, under its achieved colloidal form, to stir up antibodies in the body of the one who ingests it.

The mysterious secret preparation for the uniting of father and son - in 1923 - leaves much to reflect upon, particularly as the latter signed the death certificate of the former, in contradiction with the regulations in force that require that the doctor who performs such a funerary deed be unrelated to the deceased's family! What should then be concluded? The sagacious reader should have an inkling as to the answer...

---

[241] *Therapeutical Colloids and Anaphylaxis* (Tr.). Minutes of the Société de Biologie, Les Colloïdes, 1922.

# X
# From the Master's Succession to the "Strange Manor"

After the *official* disappearance of Fulcanelli in 1923, his disciple, Eugène Canseliet, succeeded the Master. Nine years later, one year after Julien Champagne's death in 1932, Eugène Canseliet moved to 10 quai des Célestins in Paris. His new residence was again a garret room, but this time one which was better fitted for alchemical work. He had carried out a variety of experiments the previous year - notably on the wet path. Following in the footsteps of Irenee Philalethes, he used a glass matrass in which he achieved a long coction of gold-mercury. He depicted this in a series of forty-eight watercolours, which, alas, disappeared during the invasion in 1940.

In 1932, Canseliet also became acquainted with Paul Le Cour, the chair of the *Atlantis* association, headquartered in Vincennes. He collaborated with the association for half a century, publishing numerous articles of high literary quality on the subject of hermeticism with them. Curiously, Paul Le Cour revealed to Canseliet that the famous sentence that he had heard in a dream in his adolescence:

When, in your house, black ravens have begotten white doves, then you will be called The Wise...

figured "among others also seen on the lintel, jambs and threshold of a door", which was dated 1680 and integrated into the wall enclosing the public gardens at Piazza Vittorio-Emmanuele in Rome, and which was among the last remains of Marquis Massimiliano Palombara's villa. Astounded by such a "coincidence", Eugène

Canseliet decided to undertake a thorough study of that new "philosopher's dwelling", and indeed included it in a book signed this time with his own name: *"Deux Logis Alchimiques"*[242], published by Jean Schemit in 1945. What is even more curious is that the eminent scholar through whom these inscriptions reached Eugène Canseliet was actually named Cancellieri!

In 1936, on the occasion of a party organized to celebrate the bonfire of St. John, the writer Rosny the Elder questioned Eugène Canseliet about Fulcanelli's identity. Pierre Geyraud reported this conversation in his book, *L'Occultisme à Paris*[243]:

> [...] I am only the "prefacer", answered Eugène Canseliet to his interlocutor; Champagne is only the illustrator; and Fulcanelli is the pseudonym of a third person whom, in observance of the hermetic rule of silence, I am not allowed to designate otherwise. This Fulcanelli *is still alive*. He is commissioned by the White Brotherhood to help with the evolution of mankind. He is a genuine Rose-Cross[244]. He is sometimes in Argentina, sometimes traveling all over the world in the way of the Rose-Cross of old. For the time being, he is *in the south of France*. He is a master with wonderful powers....

Was this enlightening reply from a studious disciple an authentic testimony, or was it simply reflecting a belief? Was it a figment of the imagination of an idealist imbued with mysticism? The question remains irremediably open, even and above all, if we keep in mind the time-honoured tradition of the Adepts. Did Bertrand Russell not write:

> It is good to believe certain things and bad to believe others, irrespective of the knowledge that these things are true or false! [245]

That year, Eugène Canseliet succeeded in extracting the "philosopher's sulphur", the precious *rémore*, embryo of the Philosopher's Stone. Two years later, he undertook the famous

---

[242] *Two Alchemical Dwellings* (Tr.).
[243] *Occultism in Paris*, Editions Emile-Paul Fr., 1953.
[244] See my book, *Saint Germain ... Les mystères de la Rose-Croix* (*St. Germain...The Mysteries of the Rose-Cross*), Ed. De Vecchi, 1995.
[245] Free quotation (Tr).

coction of the Third Work at Deuil-la-Barre (in the Val d'Oise area) where he had just settled with his family. When the aurora borealis arose - glowing brilliantly and exceptionally visible in the nocturnal European skies on that Monday, January 24, 1938 - the *Egg* hatched and the radiating energy, like a little Sun, suddenly arose from the athenor and rushed into the chimney.

> Anticipated apocalyptic spectacle promised by Saint John where, radiating from the north, long, green beams hit the red coat spreading in the sky that seemed to reflect all the blood that martyred mankind was about to shed on Earth....[246]

It should be mentioned that, indeed, a few months later, the Second World War broke out!

Canseliet attempted to produce the famous coction again three times after that, but was, alas, always unsuccessful.

In the 1950s, he went on a very unusual trip to Spain, the story of which he *secretly* confided to his friend, writer Claude Seignolle. Seignolle wanted to publish this strange story in a compendium of more or less fantastic tales, and ultimately yielded to the temptation to do so, though he did so under conditions of the strictest anonymity. The book appeared in 1969 under the generic title "*Invitation au Château de l'Etrange*[247]":

> By revealing this confidential adventure, I am going to betray a friend with whom there has been a strong exchange of affection going on for a long time - not only with him, but also with his two daughters. He is a simple, modest, and - this goes without saying - sincere man. His science is vast, genuine. Of course, I will keep his name secret, for he is famous and respected in esoteric circles, but I bend my head before his reproaches in advance, in case he should see these lines.
>
> Every day, he receives a minister's correspondence and he regularly exchanges exciting letters with, among others, a rich Castilian family. This family claims to be withdrawn from Time, and writes in an old French delightfully interspersed with imperfect subjunctives,

---

[246] *Les Deux Logis Alchimique.*
[247] *Invitation to a Strange Castle* (Tr), Editions Maisonneuve et Larose.

to the great joy of my friend who speaks this way on a daily basis, even with his grocer.

Two or three years ago, these Castilians sent him a plane ticket to Madrid, inviting him to spend a few days with them in order to learn more from him, and themselves pledging to teach him more about his specialty - which actually seemed to be a challenge! The adventure being tempting, my friend, although little inclined to accept that kind of invitation, felt he was on the verge of discovering interesting things. Indeed, already, the style and contents of the letters received over several years never failed to surprise him by their subtle remarks, as well as by their rich contributions.

He took the plane. At the Madrid airport, an old Hispano car was waiting for him. The chauffeur looked more like a coachman than a driver, wearing an old-fashioned livery and looking worthy of appearing in one of Goya's paintings. Nobody else came to welcome him and the chauffeur remained silent. My friend began one of his usual smiling meditations as he enjoyed the ride. They covered a long distance and at dusk arrived before the gates of a park enclosed by high walls. However, they had not yet reached their destination: a sinuous, stony road led them first to the left, then to the right, as if losing itself.... At last they stopped along a platform. The driver turned off the engine, got out, and taking my friend's suitcase, invited him to follow him. There, a lane led them farther. They walked for a long time before arriving at a large, old mansion, low but stately.

Upon entering, my friend observed that there was no electricity. No bulbs. Here, the only light came from candles. Was it in his honour, to give an atmosphere of old-Spain? Or was it customary? His hosts were there waiting for him, faithful to a dressing tradition that, instead of leading him to consider it a grotesque masquerade, gave him cause to rejoice. "At last," he thought, "here are people who know how to evade this century's ever-changing and sometimes daring fashions. Here, all the ladies are wearing long dresses. Velvets and brocades. The gentlemen are wearing a kind of doublet, long stockings, buckle shoes."

All gathered around the Master come from another place and welcomed him (for an instant I place myself in that delightful man's stead when he heard old-French, peppered with old-Castilian, spoken around him).

The welcoming repast had the same old-fashioned flavour, regarding both the food, as well as the service. As for conversation, it was quite astonishing. My friend soon noticed - which he had already observed from their letters - that his hosts, while not quite sure of themselves in the field of modern alchemy, had a thorough knowledge of ancient alchemy, and spoke about it quite naturally, just as they would about things that they would normally do on a daily basis. My friend was then stupefied to hear - since he believed that he knew everything - not only of the existence of books of which he was unaware and the quoting of forgotten formulas, but also of the existence of the lost Force of ancient alchemy, which he found in these people.

Who were these characters living in 1966, but who were keeping the lifestyle of the eighteenth-century? He carefully refrained from asking. In any case, had he not seen even stranger things in his magician's life?

His sojourn there lasted one week. Not only did he learn a lot, but it was a beneficial recovery cure. He saw planes crossing the sky *without the slightest noise*, and on the neighbouring road, *cars drove in silence*, as if the present was only a figment of his imagination. There were no sounds around him other than the ones of a loving and peaceful family indefatigably and patiently repeating their daily gestures and holding the feverish conversations of an endless life.

Of course, Eugène Canseliet heard about the publication of this singular tale, and two years later in 1971, decided to speak about the strange trip that had brought him to the surroundings of Seville. Journalist Henri Rode took his statement in an interview that the good master of Savignies gave to the magazine *Le Grand Albert* (n°1):

As for Fulcanelli, alive, he certainly is… Time does not matter… It so happens that I saw him again in 1951 and I discovered the secret place where he is. I was traveling in Spain, not far from Seville, where I was the guest of a friend who owns a beautiful mansion with a terrace and large staircase opening on a park. I immediately felt Fulcanelli in the atmosphere. The more so as I discovered from my window - which added to the charm of the picture - the presence of a child of about 10 and a little girl, who both seemed to have originated from a painting by Velazquez. A pony and two greyhounds were at their sides. But after one of those long working nights so customary for me, my discovery seemed even more convincing: in a large lane with dense foliage, a young lady, a queen, was approaching, wearing the Collar of the Golden Fleece and was followed by a Duenna. All this very vivid, very luminous. The young lady warmly nodded to me, and I was sure that Fulcanelli whispered, "Do you recognize me?", to which I replied, "Yes". But how could such certainties be conveyed?

Edifying testimony indeed!

Let us add some excerpts from the book by Kenneth Rayner Johnson, entitled *The Fulcanelli Phenomenon: The Story of a Twentieth-Century Alchemist in the Light of New Examination of the Hermetic Tradition*[248]:

> Eugène Canseliet, the man who was closest to Fulcanelli, all during his strange existence, affirmed that again he saw his master in Spain at a more recent date: 1954.[249]

Kenneth Rayner Johnson says he is sure of the quoted date:

> Undoubtedly, Mr Canseliet was in Spain during this year. Gérard Heym, a knowledgeable esoterist, knew M. Canseliet through his friendship with his daughter and was able to see Canseliet's passport. It contained a visa for Spain only for 1954.

This checking indeed leaves no room for doubt. Later on we shall see why this is so important to us. For the time being, let us continue with the British author's story:

> Mr Canseliet prepared his bags and undertook his trip to Spain. His destination was Seville. [...] Someone came to meet him – we don't know exactly who – and M. Canseliet was conduced to a manor or a large estate in the mountains. There he was received by his old master, Fulcanelli, who appeared to be about fifty. M. Canseliet was fifty-four.
>
> M. Canseliet was taken to his rooms, on the first floor, in a tower of the manor; the window opened on a large, rectangular terrace. During his stay, he had the distinct impression that the manor was the refuge of an entire colony of distinguished alchemists—including Adepts like his master—and that it was owned by Fulcanelli. Shortly after

---

[248] Publisher, Neville Spearman, Jersey, 1980.
[249] Retranslated from the French. (Tr.)

his arrival, he was shown to a small laboratory and was told he could work there and carry on his experiments.

Returning to his rooms, M Canseliet went to his window to breathe some fresh air and observed the patio below. He saw a group of children—probably the children of other guests at the manor—who were playing. But there was something strange about them. In looking more closely, he realized it was in the clothing they were wearing. They looked like they were from the XVIth century. The children were playing some sort of game, and M. Canseliet thought they were dressed this way for a masquerade or a costume party. That night he went to bed without thinking more about the incident.

The next day, he returned to his experiments in the laboratory he had been given. From time to time his master visited him briefly to watch over his progress.

One morning, M. Canseliet, descending the staircase of the tower in which he was staying, found himself under a vaulted porch that opened onto the patio when, suddenly, he heard voices. Crossing the patio, he approached a group of three women who were talking animatedly. M. Canseliet was surprised to see that they were wearing ample and long clothes in the style of the XVIth century, just like the children he had seen two days earlier. Was it another masquerade? The women then approached him. M. Canseliet was torn between surprise at what he was seeing and embarrassment at being dressed so casually. He went to turn around and return to his rooms when, as the women passed by, one of them turned abruptly, looked at him, and gave him a smile.

All this lasted only an instant. The woman rejoined her companions and together they continued on, out of sight. [...]

M. Canseliet remained shaken because he could have sworn that the face of the woman who had given him the smile was that of Fulcanelli...

What can be concluded from the above? That she was closely related to the Adept? Or else, as Kenneth Rayner Johnson suggests, was it an initiatory phenomenon comparable to a shamanic trance, and in this case, perfectly symbolizing the archetype of the hermetic androgynous state?

In any event, the prodigious character of these experiences as reported by Eugène Canseliet certainly deserves further consideration.

Indeed, he gave further details in various interviews. He revealed in *Le Feu du Soleil* that:

> He [Fulcanelli] is no longer there. He is on the Earth, but it is the Earthly Paradise. What does he do now? I have seen nothing. I saw him upon my arrival, when he welcomed me in a three-piece suit. […]
>
> And then I saw him while I was working in the laboratory. He came to see me where I was working, and I saw him; I saw him twice. […]
>
> When they came to fetch me, they said it was to go to Italy. Upon arrival in Paris, we stopped in front of the Drouant restaurant, Gare de l'Est. At that time, it took at least three days to obtain a visa for Spain. They went to fetch my visa and brought it back at once. So, we were to travel to Spain. It was near Seville. I was walking like a king. All that was needed was there, but I always went back to my apartment and left again early every morning. There were apple and lemon trees in the garden, and a brisk stream. It was magnificent!
>
> So, I certainly did not expect to meet Fulcanelli with my suspenders falling down on my trousers. When he saw me, he again addressed me as "tu" and "toi", as he used to do: "But then, you (tu) recognize me?"
>
> It is difficult to recognize a child you have known when he is 25. In this case, it was the opposite. The previous times I had seen Fulcanelli in the Sarcelles gasworks, for instance, he was a handsome old man, but an old man. But I recognized him because I had drawn portraits.

And then on Jacques Chancel's *Radioscopie* radio programme in 1978:

> It is as if he had gone backwards in Time, but one still recognizes many things in the face: ears, the shape, the hair, greying, yes, but which was black. Well, you will tell me that he could be dyeing it! No, it was him. I could not see whether or not he had new teeth, I am going far, but on the whole, what bearing!...

To this should be added a posthumous testimony, supplied this time by the late Jean Laplace. Shortly after Eugène Canseliet's demise in 1982, Laplace and Eugène Canseliet's daughter, Isabelle, discovered a cardboard folder in the family house in Savignies. This folder contained documents pertaining to the famous *Finis Gloriae*

*Mundi* - Fulcanelli's unpublished third book - as well as a precious relic connected to the mysterious trip to Seville, which he alluded to as follows:

> [...] A small, rectangular photographic card, serrated at the edges, as was the custom in the 1950s. I am so impressed by what this venerable relic represents that I dare not reveal its existence... What to do with it? Destroy it? It would be a shame to relegate to the ashes forever the majestic spirit fixed on a plate that is sensitive to all which irradiates.

Then in a footnote:

> It must not be thought that it is the impression of an ectoplasm. I am simply talking about the face of an ordinary mortal that has kept a human shape, and that has been enriched by an indescribable expression.

And he added:

> At Savignies, in the ground floor study after supper, an amazing silence suddenly settled. Taking the photograph in her hand with the greatest respect, Isabelle said: "I have no doubt".

And he concluded:

> [...] I think I should make it clear that the photograph referred to is no longer in the possession of any being living in this world. That was, by the way, the indispensable condition for Isabelle Canseliet and myself to be allowed to talk about it...[250]

Would it really have been all that surprising if Fulcanelli had said to his disciple when he met him again in Seville: *"Do not touch me!"*... thus renewing the Easter Mystery that sees the triumph of the *body of Light*, the only body worthy of glorious immortality?

Further, didn't Eugène Canseliet opportunely write about Fulcanelli's first initiator, the Adept Basile Valentin, in the preface to his major work: *Les Douze Clefs de la Philosophie*[251]:

---

[250] Jean Laplace, *Index général des Termes spéciaux, des Expressions et des Sentences propres à l'Alchimie, se rencontrant dans l'œuvre complète d'Eugène Canseliet*, Ed. J.-J. Pauvert, Paris, 1986.
[251] *The Twelve Keys to Philosophy*. (Tr.)

Of course, no more heavy-to-bear secret difficult to defend against malice and nastiness, for the Adept having shed his old human slough, who enjoys the invisibility and ubiquitousness devolved only upon the members of the Rose-Cross, as well as on those of the universal Heliopolis. Is, henceforth, oblivion not inherent in his glorified body, as it would be for the man who is freed from his very past?

It is this that the sensitive plate of the camera had caught, and which the late Jean Laplace sincerely attempted to convey to us....

To close this chapter where the fantastic is king, let us tell you that in *Le Feu du Soleil* Eugène Canseliet claimed that when he saw Fulcanelli again in Seville, the latter was at least 113 years of age. The reader will then understand, in view of the preceding chapters and of the evidence discovered by Gérard Heym in Eugène Canseliet's passport, verifying that Canseliet had travelled to Spain in 1954, that Fulcanelli could *only have been born in 1841*.... As was Jules Violle.

# XI
## *Finis Gloriae Mundi*
## The End of the Glory of the World

The third book written by Fulcanelli, which followed *Le Mystère des Cathédrales* and *Les Demeures philosophales* and was withdrawn by him from any eventual publication, was entitled *Finis Gloriae Mundi*: The End of the Glory of the World! The issue of this withdrawal, as one might suspect, must have been a serious one. Eugène Canseliet referred to it in the following terms:

> In light of the passive resignation of people turned into slaves of scientism, I understand better, after almost half a century, the firm decision made by Fulcanelli not to have his third book published...[252]

We should add that *Finis Gloriae Mundi* is also the name of an astounding painting that is kept at the Hospital de la Caridad (Hospital of Holy Charity), which is, interestingly, located in Seville, Spain!

The 220 x 216 cm oil on canvas was painted by the artist Juan de Valdès Leal in 1672. It was commissioned by Miguel de Mañara, also known as Don Juan. In the foreground of the painting, a corpse of a bishop in the advanced stages of decomposition can be seen lying in his coffin. Beside him, but lying in the opposite direction, is a knight in another coffin - whom Eugène Canseliet thought to be a member of the Order of Calatrava, the successor of the Templars. The knight, however, shows no signs of decay. His open eyes and fresh complexion leave us to understand that he rests peacefully and

---

[252] *La Tourbe des Philosophes*, n°4.

escapes any wear of time. Nearly all that look carefully at the knight recognize Don Juan himself there.

In the background, a curiously female hand bearing the mark of crucifixion emerges from the clouds holding a scale. One plate of the scale bears the inscription *nimas* (neither more), and the other *nimenos* (nor less)! To the left, at the entrance to the crypt, there is an owl - symbol of wisdom - that stands in hieratic posture and appears to be gravely weighing the situation. One also glimpses skeletons and scattered bones in the background, which serve to emphasize the already macabre character of this scene entitled *Finis Gloriae Mundi*, as indicated on the scroll lying beside the first coffin. The image of the bishop's coffin is disturbing since it certainly seems here that the Church has fallen into eternal decay, to the benefit of the only genuine "initiatory awakening" that is symbolized by the knight simulating death.

Further, the subject of the painting that is facing this one leaves no doubt whatsoever as to the subject matter since it presents death bearing the harvesting scythe. The skeleton's foot treads down on the world, symbolized by a globe. It seems to scorn the papacy by way of items representing it - the tiara and papal cross. It also appears to despise the riches of temporal power, as represented by the jewels and swords that are scattered here and there. With the index finger of its right hand, the skeleton points to the Latin sentence, *In ictu oculi (in the blink of an eye)* which, when added to the previous sentence gives us:

*The End of the Glory of the World, ... in the blink of an eye!*

In a very interesting text (alas, not available in bookshops), entrusted to us on a rainy day and entitled *Le Grand Oeuvre à tire-d'aile, du clerc adepte Pyrazel*[253][254] the author says:

---

[253] Pyrazel is, as well, also the author of a curious little alchemical manual - this one available - which is entitled, *L'Ambroisie du Soleil ou la Pierre Héroïque* (Ed. Ramatuel, 2000).

[254] *The Great Work Viewed in the Flap of a Wing*. (Tr.)

If, upon entering the well-known chapel of the Hospital of Holy Charity in Seville, the visitor's eye is immediately met by the two paintings by painter Juan de Valdès Leal, facing one another, one certainly must not forget another painting there by Murillo called, *"Charity of San Juan de Dios"*.

Although the presence of this Renaissance period saint, founder of the Brotherhood of Charity, is logical here, it is the location of the painting that constitutes its peculiarity. Indeed, juxtaposing it with Valdès Leal's amazing painting that completes the famous sentence "The End of the Glory of the World" with " in the blink of an eye", he confirms the hypothesis, cherished by Fulcanelli, of a shifting of the Earth's poles. To be convinced, a careful observation of both paintings side by side is enough, and a startling parallel will not fail to elicit surprise.

The arm of the angel coming to the rescue of Saint John of God in Murillo's painting and extending the sick man's legs, is in perfect alignment with the skeleton's shinbone in Valdès Leal's painting. Furthermore, the skeleton's left foot is placed on a globe, as if to prevent it from shifting on its axis, which is symbolized by the orientation of a sword. In addition, one can observe the perfect tilting of the ecliptic plane in relation to the equator, which does not leave room for any doubt as to the painter's intention in this composition.

As we mentioned earlier, before departing this world - alas too soon! - Jean Laplace was fortunate enough to discover in the famous cardboard folder at the house in Savignies the elements of a synopsis that would have been the basis of the Master's third book, *Finis Gloriae Mundi*. So here, concisely reproduced, are the notes, the precious contents of that folder:

### *The decline of our civilization and the fall of human societies*

*Religious disbelief and mystical belief.*
*Harmful effects of State education.*
*Abuse of pleasure due to fear of the future.*
*Present-day fetishism.*
*Symbols more powerful than in the past in the materialist conception.*
*Uncertainty about the future.*
*Overall distrust and diffidence.*
*Fashion and its revealing whims.*
*Unknown initiates are governing alone.*
*Mystery weighs upon consciences.*

### Earthly evidence of the end of the world

*The four Ages.*
*The successive cycles sealed in geological layers.*
*Fossils.*
*Vanished flora and fauna.*
*Human skeletons.*
*Asiatis.*
*Monuments of so-called pre-historical mankind.*
*Cromlechs.*
*Three-cross candelabra.*

### Cosmic causes of the upheaval

*The system of Ptolemy.*
*The Almagest.*
*Error in the Copernican system, demonstrated by the pole star.*
*Precession of the equinoxes.*
*Inclination of the Ecliptic.*
*Inexplicable variations in the magnetic pole.*
*Solar ascension at the pole zenith and return in the opposite direction, causing the reversal of the axis, the deluge and fusion at the surface of the globe.*[255]

According to Eugène Canseliet himself, some of these issues were already addressed in the concluding chapter of the final edition of *Les Demeures philosophales,* and in the second edition of *Le Mystère des Cathédrales* (that of 1957) with the study of the "Cyclic Cross of Hendaye".

It is true that in *Les Demeures philosophales,* the final chapter entitled, "Paradoxe illimité des sciences"[256] addresses the end of the world - or rather of a world - it being understood that is about a cycle, an era, or even a civilization, which is - as Paul Valéry stated it - no doubt a mortal one!

---

[255] Excerpt from article by Jean Laplace, "Aperçu vitriolique"– *La Tourbe des Philosophes,* N°31
[256] *Unlimited Paradox of Sciences.* (Tr.)

That chapter of *Les Demeures philosophales* begins with discussions of the "reign of Man" and the "cyclical theory of the four Ages".

## The Reign of Man

After dealing with the sad paradox of the "unlimited progress of the sciences", Fulcanelli pores over the study of a painting on sculpted wood in the church in Figeac (Lot department). Here he sees in the purposeful arrangement of the instruments of Christ's Passion, the presence of four Greek Xs (Khi), the total numerical value of which is 2,400, and which symbolize the four Ages of the world. According to his idea, the twelve centuries symbolize the Reign of God, which is succeeded by the Reign of the Son of Man.

## The Deluge

Here Fulcanelli addresses the question of the deluge universally dealt with by all religions, as well as the prospect of a new cataclysm. He makes it clear that:

> When, to punish Mankind for its crimes, God resolved to draw it into the waters of the Flood, not only was the Earth affected on the surface, but a certain number of righteous and elected people, having found mercy in His eyes, survived the flood.
>
> Although presented symbolically, he adds, this teaching rests on a positive basis. We recognize in it the physical need for an animal and terrestrial regeneration which, consequently, cannot result in the total annihilation of all creatures, nor in the elimination of any of the conditions indispensable to the life of the rescued core. Hence, despite its apparent universality, despite the terrifying and the long brewing of the elements unleashed, we are assured that the immense catastrophe will not have the same impact everywhere, nor on the entire span of continents and seas. Certain privileged regions, actual rocky arches, will shelter the men who will find a refuge there. There, during a day lasting two centuries, the generations - anguished spectators of the effects of the Divine Force - will witness the colossal duel between water and fire. There, in relative calm, in a uniform temperature, under the pale and steady light of a low sky, the

elected people will wait for peace to be made, for the last clouds - scattered by the breeze of the Golden Age - to uncover for them the polychrome magic of a double rainbow, the glittering of new skies, and the charm of a *new Earth*...

After which, Fulcanelli alludes to the various topographical changes that occurred after the last Flood, among others, the fact that Jersey Island was still attached to the Cotentin region in 709, the year when the Channel's waters invaded the vast forest that spanned as far as Ouessant, and which sheltered several villages.

**Atlantis**

Here Fulcanelli lists the numerous arguments in favour of the existence of the mysterious continent referred to by the philosopher Plato: *Atlantis*. The Adept suggests that this civilization must have reached the ultimate point:

> This high degree that God seems to have fixed as the end of human progress: "You shall go no further". Limits beyond which the symptoms of decadence manifest themselves, the fall is more pronounced if ruin is not sped up by the sudden eruption of an unforeseen catastrophe.[257]

According to Fulcanelli, a new Flood took place four thousand eight hundred years later, this time flooding the major part of North Africa:

> But more favored than the land of the Atlanean, Egypt gained from a raising of the bottom of the ocean and came back to the light of day, after a certain time of immersion. For Algeria and Tunisia with their dry "chotts" covered with a thick layer of salt, the sahara and Egypt with their soils constituted for a large part of sea sand show that the waters invaded and covered vast expanses of the African continent.[258]

Further on in the text Fulcanelli says that the cyclical cataclysm occurs alternately by water and by fire, in the same hemisphere.

---

[257] *Dwellings*, p. 512.
[258] Ibid.

Regarding this, Jean Laplace found in the "famous cardboard folder" that was discovered in the Savignies house after Eugène Canseliet's demise, an enigmatic text entitled, *"Fire"*, of which we give the *in fine* content below, which expounds upon our topic enormously:

> One knows that since the highest Antiquity, fire has always been *represented by a triangle* with the summit above, that is to say, pointing upward, and with its base below. As a matter of fact, this geometrical shape is the shape of a flame of fire in action, and one which belongs to all pyramids. This would lead us to see in the Dammartin-sous-Tigeaux pyramid (Seine-et-Marne), as well as in the Memphis one, etc. monuments that were erected in anticipation of a catastrophe by fire.
>
> Hence, the Egyptians would have built those immense edifices, not only with a view to making them geodesic witnesses meant to transmit to posterity the accurate, mathematical knowledge that they possessed about our world at the time, but also as signs intended to inform mankind of the inescapable necessity for it to be renewed by fire.
>
> Those ancestors of our current civilizations had, via the successive fates of our Earth, a knowledge so thorough that they carved their hypogeums in the rock and their necropoles in absolutely waterproof subterranean halls. Those men indeed knew that they themselves would perish by water. By elevating their pyramids above the ground, it was for us, their successors, that they were working since they did not fear fire, but water.
>
> Also, the word pyramid contains this meaning. In Greek, *pyramis* (πυραμις) comes from *pyr*, *pyros* (πυρ, πυρος), that is, "fire", and *amis*, roots; *ami* (αμι) sickle; *pyrame* is then, the harvester's sickle. And this singularly sheds light on the awe-inspiring, but correct sentences in the Scriptures,
>
> "Let the nations be roused; let them advance into the Valley of Jehoshaphat, for there I will sit to judge all the nations on every side."
>
> "Swing the sickle, for the harvest is ripe. Come, trample the grapes, for the wine press is full and the vats overflow- so great is their wickedness!"
>
> "The sun and moon will be darkened, and the stars no longer shine." (Joel 3, v. 12, 13, 15)

Moreover, Saint John also wrote in his Apocalypse:

"Then I heard a voice from heaven say, 'Write: Blessed are the dead who die in the Lord from now on.'"

'Yes,' says the Spirit, 'they will rest from their labour, for their deeds will follow them.'

"I looked, and there before me was a white cloud, and seated on the cloud was one 'like a son of man with a crown of gold on his head and a sharp sickle in his hand"[259].

But it should be added – again according to Jean Laplace - that there was also a photograph in the cardboard file that might have served as Jean-Julien Champagne's model for the design of the frontispiece for *Finis Gloriae Mundi*, which had a handwritten note on the back explaining that the round curve of the frame should be inserted on one side of the flooded and submerged Pyramids of Egypt, with the Greek word *chthes* (χθες = yesterday) written on a scroll, and on the other side, similar pyramids in a calcinated landscape, with the word *aurion* (αυριον = tomorrow), likewise written on a scroll.

**The Burning**

In this chapter, Fulcanelli mentions the fact that the first book of the Bible, Genesis, tells the story of the Flood, and likewise, the Apocalypse at the end closes the holy book with the flames of the Last Judgement. In his opinion, it is the cyclical theory of the end, alternately brought about by water and by fire, that is intentionally emphasized here. He quotes Saint Peter's second epistle:

> |..."By these waters also the world of that time was deluged and destroyed."
>
> "By the same word, the present heavens and earth are reserved for fire, being kept for the day of judgment and destruction of ungodly men [...]"[260].

---

[259] Revelation, Saint-John, Apocalypse 14, v. 13-14.
[260] Peter, 2 – v. 6, 7.

Fulcanelli sees, in a noble equestrian statue located under a semi-circular arch on the porch of the Melle church in the Deux-Sèvres region, a representation of the Knight of the Apocalypse, where the Son of Man is identified as Christ the King, come to judge the living and the dead.

Further on, the Adept describes the obelisk located in Dammartin-sous-Tigeaux, erected on a mound in the Crécy forest. It is erected at the centre of the crossing of three roads, which gives it the appearance of a six-point star representing the Philosopher's Stone, as well as the union of fire and water. It is in fact:

> ... of a trunk made of a quadrangular pyramid with furrowed edges; indeed an amortizement in which the whole interest of the building is concentrated. In fact, it shows planet earth delivered onto the united forces of fire and water. Resting on the waves of a furious sea, the sphere of the world, struck at the upper pole by the Sun during its helical reversing movement, is set ablaze and propels thunderbolts and lightning. That is, as we said, the amazing representation of the immense fire and flood, which is as purifying as it is retributive.

## The Golden Age

It is by way of a sublime reference that Fulcanelli reveals to us the path to the Golden Age:

> In the period of the Golden Age, Man, rejuvenated, ignores all religion. He only gives thanks to the Creator of whom the Sun, his most sublime creation, seems to reflect His blazing, luminous, and bountiful image. He respects, honours and worships God in this radiant globe that is the intellect and heart of Nature, and the supplier of earthly goods. Visible representative of the Eternal, the Sun is also the sentient token of His Power, His grandeur and His kindness. Within the star's beams, under the pure skies of a rejuvenated Earth, Man admires the divine achievements, without external manifestations, without rites and without veils. Contemplative, unaware of necessity, desire, suffering, he holds for the Master of the Universe the heartfelt and deep gratitude possessed by the simple soul, and the boundless affection binding the Son to His Father.

Fulcanelli then develops the notion of an "earthly paradise", alluding, in passing, to its Chaldean root - *pardes* - meaning a delightful garden, one which man has often attempted to locate upon our planet. However, this search has been in vain and for a good reason, states Fulcanelli, who takes this opportunity to back up his cyclical thesis with the following:

> The rescue and mercy zone is in the boreal hemisphere at the beginning of one cycle, then in the austral hemisphere, at the beginning of the following cycle.

The Adept concludes by associating the Four Ages of the Great Year, as he refers to it, to the four respective seasons composing the solar year: spring, summer, fall and winter.

And so ends *Les Demeures philosophales*.

**The Cyclic Cross of Hendaye**

As Eugène Canseliet made clear, the symbolic interpretation of the "Hendaye cross" relates to the notes that accompanied the manuscript of *Finis Gloriae Mundi*. Its publication in the second edition of *Le Mystère des Cathédrales* is quite significant in this respect.

Most probably erected at the end of the seventeenth century, this modest stone cross on the frontier of the Basque region is adorned with highly symbolic elements. Fulcanelli tells us:

> The Hendaye Cross proves by the ornamentation of its pedestal that it is the most unusual monument of primitive millenarianism, the rarest symbolic translation of chiliasm, that we have ever come across. It is known that this doctrine - first accepted and then rejected by Origen, Saint Denys of Alexandria and Saint Jerome, although not condemned by the Church - was part of the esoteric tradition of the ancient philosophy of Hermes.[261]

On the transversal beam of the cross, one reads the common Latin inscription:

O CRUX AVE SPES UNICA

But it is arranged here in a very unusual way:

*OCRUXAVES*<br>*PESUNICA*

---

[261] *Le Mystère des Cathédrales*, pg. 166 (English version).

Why did the sculptor join the letters composing this Latin sentence, although so common, unless it was to veil a more mysterious meaning, where the S (of AVES) seems to play a major role:

> The letter S, writes *the Adept*, which has the sinuous shape of a snake, corresponds to the Greek X (khi) and assumes its esoteric meaning. It is the spiral track of the Sun arrived at the zenith of its curve across space, during the time of the cyclical catastrophe. It is a theoretical image of the Beast of the Apocalypse, of the dragon, which on the Day of Judgement, spews out fire and brimstone upon the macrocosmic creation. Thanks to the symbolic value of the letter S, which is displaced on purpose, we understand that the inscription must be translated into a secret language, that is to say, in *the language of the gods* or *the language of the birds*, and that its meaning must be discovered with the help of the rules of *Diplomacy*. Several authors, and in particular Grasset d'Orcet, in his analysis of *Le Songe de Poliphile*[262] published by the *Revue Britannique*, have explained these clearly enough for us to dispense with repeating them.[263]

Therefore, the Latin sentence should be translated into French, and its vowels shifted according to the cabbalistic rule quoted by the original archaeologist, in order to obtain the following sentence, which is pregnant with meaning of great import:

> Il est écrit que la vie se réfugie en un seul espace[264]

And Fucanelli adds:

> For the elite, the children of Elijah, will be saved according to the word of the Scriptures, because their profound faith, their untiring perseverance in effort, will have earned for them the right to be promoted to the rank of disciples of the Christ-Light.[265]

Furthermore, there is a different symbol on each face of the pedestal. The Sun, the Moon, an eight-point star and a cross surrounded by four Greek Alphas designating the four Ages of the world.

---

[262] *Poliphile's dream* (Tr.).
[263] *Le Mystère des Cathédrales*, pg. 167-68 (English version).
[264] It is written that life takes refuge in a single place (Tr.). Ibid., pg. 168 (English version).
[265] Ibid.

Consequently, at the risk of once again vexing Geneviève Dubois, we must say that the article written by Jules Boucher in 1936 for the periodical *Constellation* on the enigmatic Hendaye cross is far from having the same value of the chapter on this cross so meticulously written by Fulcanelli *in illo tempore*. For example, what should be kept of the following astounding (and absurd) statement excerpted from Jules Boucher's text?

*The Sun Dial at Holyrood in Edinborough.*

*Contrary to the testimony of Mme. Dubois, it is indeed possible to visit this monument discussed by Fulcanelli, as the above photograph taken by the author illustrates!*

Which means that the North Pole will become the South Pole, and conversely, when the devouring Sun (please refer to our article on the Black Sun), having reached the culminating point of its course, will travel in the opposite direction while keeping the same direction of rotation.[266]

On the other hand, Geneviève Dubois, who is not averse to imprecision, had already claimed regarding the above text excerpted from the second edition of *Les Demeures philosophales*, which referred to the burning of the northern hemisphere, that this excerpt referred to the burning of the Planet (Dubois, op. cit. p. 184). Likewise, as we have mentioned twice, it is indeed the chapter on the Cyclic Cross of Hendaye that did not appear in the first edition of *Les Mystères des Cathédrales*, and *not* the section entitled "*Paradoxe illimité des Progrès des Sciences*", which was missing in the *princeps* edition of *Les Demeures philosophales*, as she incorrectly states (op. cit. pp. 176-184). I am also prepared, whenever she wishes, to very easily arrange for her to see the celebrated Holyrood Palace sundial in Edinburgh, contrary to her erroneous allegations that it is not available to the public (op. cit. p. 176), since I had the opportunity to see it for ourselves.

But let us return to our previous concerns and ask some questions. As incredible as they sound, could the theories expressed by Fulcanelli about the cyclical shifting of the poles be scientifically tenable, or should they be considered *chimeras*?

Surely, our Adept had heard *in illo tempore* about the works of Goguel on the age-old shifting of the poles, of Milankovic and his theory based on the hypothesis that the globe is a distortable mass[267], and of Verhandelingen's theory that the shifting of the poles is partly due to secondary 21,000-year loops (of the Sun and of the precessions)[268]. We will recall that this question of precessions was alluded to in the synopsis of *Finis Gloriae Mundi*. Was it not stated:

---

[266] Op Cit., Dubois

[267] He was in disagreement with astronomer Schiaparelli who had written in 1889: "The Globe is supposed to be of an absolute rigidity, the poles can undergo variations of only a fraction of a degree under the effect of geological actions."

[268] In *Mémoires de l'Académie royale des Sciences d'Outre-Mer* (Memoranda to the Overseas Academy of Sciences. (Tr.).

Error in the Copernican system, demonstrated by the polar star. Precessions of the equinoxes, ...

What could this mean, exactly? Obviously, it had to do with the astronomical phenomenon, now recognized, that the Earth does not only perform the two types of rotation described by Copernicus: spinning and rotation around the Sun. In truth, it performs several others, among which is the famous precession that can be briefly described as follows.

The Earth's axis of rotation achieves a conical motion, which is very slow, but also has significant effects. Further, the Earth is not quite spherical, but has an ellipsoidal shape due to a bulging at the equator. Due to this and to some other factors, the gravitational attractions exerted by the Moon and the Sun tend to cause a tilting of the axis of rotation, which causes it to merge with the axis of the ecliptic. However, the Earth resists these attracting forces, and the determining element of this resistance is its spinning motion. This conflict consequently triggers a complex system of forces that pull in different directions. The Earth's axis (with a current tilt of 23°30') is thus forced to perform a circular motion around the axis of the ecliptic with which it is, so to speak, coupled at the level of the Centre of the Earth. Hence the conical motion that could be compared to the motion of a spinning top.

The conical motion characterizing the precession takes place counter-clockwise, relative to the north. Its speed is steady and it lasts about 25,920 years - the great Platonic year. One consequence of this is a slow shifting of each celestial pole that describes, on the celestial sphere, a circle with an angular radius of 23°30'. This explains the change in the "polar star" that we have seen many times on Earth. Was it not located in the Draco Constellation long before being in Ursa Minor?

After this necessary digression, let us come back to the scientific studies regarding the thorny issue of pole shifts. Precursor geophysicists P. David (in 1904) and B. Brunhes (in 1906) were studying volcanic lava flows of the Quaternary period in the Puys[269] range of the central Massif when they observed that the magnetic

---

[269] A "puy" is a dormant volcano (Tr.).

direction of some of the flows was different from what it should have been for that period. Taking into account that a few years earlier their colleague, G. Folgerhaiter, had suggested that the remnant magnetization of iron oxides in volcanic rocks and of the ambient magnetic field were identical, both geophysicists concluded there had been a pole shift during the course of time. This was confirmed by the development of the potassium-argon isotope (K-Ar) dating method using a mass spectrometer, which provided a degree of accuracy, until then unimaginable, within just a few dozen millennia. Further, at the beginning of the 1960s, both Americans and Australians suggested chronological scales for geomagnetic polarization, which gave the succession of the inversions that occurred in the last five million years[270]. Nowadays, this phenomenon is well-known among scientists, and studied most meticulously.

We can only conclude that, once again, Fulcanelli was able to emphasize a crucial point in physics, which is widely confirmed nowadays, this time regarding magnetism and geomagnetism. This is particularly meaningful as we are now seeing the gradual fading of our terrestrial magnetic field, which precedes an impending pole shift[271].

**Regarding a Forged *Finis Gloriae Mundi***

At the end of 1999, a book with this title and signed "Fulcanelli" was published by a London publishing house for fiscal reasons, followed by an aggressive advertising campaign. However, the book met with general indifference, for the readers noted the lack of generous prose and considerable erudition that is characteristic of the real Fulcanelli! Moreover, the said document was diametrically opposed to the synopsis of the genuine *Finis Gloriae Mundi*. To explain this further, we will now borrow a few pertinent criticisms

---

[270] Cf. "Quand le nord était au sud" ("When the North was at the South". Tr.). *La Recherche* (June 1990) and "Les inversions du champ magnétique terrestre" ("Inversions of Earth's Magnetic Field"), by J. P. Valet ad V. Courtillot, *La Recherche* (n°246, 1992).
[271] Cf. also *Alchimie: Science et Mystique* (op.cit.), chapter dedicated to "l'Alchimie de la Terre" ("The Alchemy of the Earth") where there is a reference to "Chandler oscillations" and to the phenomenon of the "nutation" of the Earth's axis.

excerpted from J. P. Thomas' article, *Finis Gloriae Mundi: Or The Story of Character Impersonation and Usurpation:*

[…] Last hypothesis: It is believed that the "prefacer" and the publisher did not even bother to read this stupid manuscript, which was sent to them either via the Internet and their e-mail, as they so claim, or by ordinary mail. Imagine Fulcanelli expressing himself on the Web after some 70 years of absence and having then reached the old age of 103!!! But the reader can be rest assured, this Fulcanelli is much younger indeed.[…]

What a lack of respect for the sagacious reader, thus despised, and whose credulousness seems not to be held in doubt, if those pernicious plotters are to be believed! Surely they must possess certified, expert qualifications and flawless insight for having granted their imprimatur to such a collection of "politico-chemical" ineptitudes in which the authentic Science of Hermes is so conspicuous ….. by its absence!

Should, despite all this, the publisher (Savary) and the author (Jacques d'Arès) of the dithyrambic preface to the book in question manage to be relieved from all responsibility and obvious duplicity, it would, however, remain that the subject of the offence is still inexorably a forged Fulcanelli…

[…] From the start the author makes things very clear: "This book is not the manuscript we once withdrew from the hands of our dear Canseliet; that old, imperfect work would but have misled the seeker, as was the case for us for a while; that was remorselessly delivered to the fire. […] It is not enough to have made some potable gold capable of inverting the physiological effects of an atomic irradiation to be able to remodel the universe to one's own taste. (p. 38)

The more than audacious comparisons between the eagle associated with the American emblem and the philosophical Eagles or alchemical sublimations of the Second Work provide upsetting images of an extreme debility. Our dabbler in "politico-alchemy" did indeed outdo himself. Here is a small example: "Parallel to the Emerald Tablet, the false demiurges used other alchemical texts without understanding them better. Why did President Truman desire a cold war that Stalin did not want at the time, if not for the reason that his councillors had read the comments on the battle between the two natures at the opening of the matter? Why did they not pursue their reading to the end! (pp. 79-80).

In conclusion, J. P. Thomas wrote regarding this grotesque parody:

> The wise reader should be advised to avoid unnecessarily spending his time and money by not buying a book so obnoxious and underhanded in the second place, and ridiculous and insipid in the first place![272]

---

[272] See our internet site: http://www.alchymie.net.

*Juan de Valdés Leal:* Finis Gloriae Mundi

*Can we suggest a relationship between the title of the famous third volume of Fulcanelli, never published, and the paintings found in the Hospital of Saint Charity in Seville, the city to which Eugène Canseliet voyaged in 1954 for his last meeting with his Master?*

*Juan de Valdés Leal:* In Ictu Oculi

*Murillo:* St. John of God carrying a sick man

*Finis Gloriae Mundi* 175

*Jean de Valdés Leal:* D. Miguel Mañara, Leyendo la regal de la Caridad.
*Hermetic symbols abound in this work. Mañara appears to be pointing to the painting of the globe going up in smoke.*

*Close-up of face from* St. John of God.
*Note the resemblance to the above portrait of D. Miguel Mañara.*

*The author showing the relationship between* In Ictu Oculi *and St. John of God carrying a sick man in the chapel of Saint Charity*

"If, in the ostentatious baroque church of the Hospital of Saint Charity in Seville, it is the two paintings facing one another by Jean de Valdés Leal that attract the the eye of the visitor upon entering, we must not forget the canvas by Murillo, entitled St. John of God carries a sick man. Even if the presence of this Renaissance saint, founder of the Brothers of Charity, is logical here, it is the placement of the painting that is singular. Its juxtaposition with the striking painting of Valdés Leal that finishes the famous sentence The End of the Glory of the World *by* In the Blink of an Eye *clearly reinforces the hypothesis, dear to Fulcanelli, of the displacement of the earth's poles. To be persuaded, it suffices to observe the two paintings side by side, where the striking parallels cannot but surprise the observer.*

*The right arm of the angel coming to aid St. John of God, extending the legs of the sick man, of Murillo's painting, is perfectly in alignment with the tibias of the skeleton in the painting by Valdés Leal. The left foot of the skeleton is moreover placed on the globe of the earth, as if he is restraining it from tipping on its axis, symbolized by the orientation of the sword. We remark as well the perfect inclination of the level of the ecliptic vis-à-vis the equator, which leaves no doubt as to the intentions of the painter of this composition.*"

    *Pyrazel:* Le Grand Oeuvre à tire-d'aile, du clerc adepte Pyrazel

# XII
## Eugène Canseliet's Alchemical Memoirs

After settling in Savignies (near Beauvais) in 1946, Eugène Canseliet carried on Fulcanelli's work by publishing numerous articles in the periodicals *Atlantis* and *Initiation et Science* (among others). He brought some of them together and had them published in a book: *Alchimie* (Editions J. J. Pauvert, 1964). He then published comments accompanying the *Mutus Liber*[273]. Publisher Pauvert later republished Fulcanelli's books and published Eugène Canseliet's key book: *L'Alchimie expliquée sur ses Textes classiques*[274], in 1972. In this document, he actually reaches the apotheosis of his teachings, with an unequalled mastery of speech. He personally considered that this work provided both a major analysis and synthesis of his literary works. Thus, he became the *de facto* leader of the informal school that grouped together all of those seriously interested in the art of Hermes. As an example, I provide a short passage below from a letter he addressed to the author shortly after the publication of his book:

---

[273] Editions J. J. Pauvert, 1967
[274] *Alchemy Explained By Its Classic Texts.* (Tr.)

It is certain that a reading, or rather the study, of *Alchemy Explained by its Classic Texts* would answer your letter. Do you possess the work?

Regarding another matter, the reader undoubtedly must have noticed in our study - which is more of an investigation than a biography - that some of Eugène Canseliet's remarks about Fulcanelli were often inconsistent, and even sometimes contradictory - for instance, in the chronology of the stories. In our opinion, this was not due to old age, but rather for a major and essential reason: "unveiling" in order to be better able to "veil" later on, if need be[275], thus making the unequivocal identification of Fulcanelli practically impossible! Hence, there are some misgivings about the celebrated "transmutation" that took place at the Sarcelles gasworks: was it in 1922 or in 1921, the very year when Eugène Canseliet had worked on Vigenère's "little particular"?

The problem arose again with respect to the date of the famous "trip to Spain": did it take place in 1951, 1952, 1954, or even 1966 (if we are to take Claude Seignolle's tale into account)? Further, was the destination of that trip Madrid or Castile or Seville, as we have good reason to think it was?

Actually, Eugène Canseliet purposely sent the reader on the wrong trail as far as Fulcanelli's identification is concerned. To one truth confessed was immediately added an untruth. Here is a blatant example: when he declared to Robert Amadou (*Le Feu du Soleil*) that in the year of the trip to Spain, Fulcanelli had reached 113 years of age, he was telling the truth - his master being born in 1841- since it is now confirmed, thanks to the visa on his passport, that the trip could have only taken place in 1954, and not in 1951 or 1952, as sometimes indicated by Eugène Canseliet, who was, on those occasions, being deliberately misleading.

Now, as far as the year 1919 is concerned, when Fulcanelli and his disciple met fortuitously at the de Lesseps town-house and the latter made a remark about his paternal grandmother's demise at the age of 80, Fulcanelli is supposed to have exclaimed: "Well, exactly

---

[275] It must be added that this process is often used by alchemists in their writings.

*Eugène Canseliet in his Savignies laboratory*

my age!". But Eugène Canseliet carefully failed to point out that *his grandmother had died on January 1st of that year.* So, unless she was born on the first day of the year 1839, she could only be in her eightieth year, i.e. she was only 79.

Eugène Canseliet stated that the meeting with his master had taken place in the autumn, but the odds are poor that it was in the second half of November when Fulcanelli, having just celebrated his birthday, was also starting his seventy-ninth year. In conclusion, Eugène Canseliet's paternal grandmother and our hermetic savant were practically the same age, although it would be quite impossible to determine the latter's age accurately if we only take into consideration the "eighty years old" mentioned by the disciple, which was, we will admit, quite adroit on his part.

We wanted to make this clear so that our possible detractors cannot object to these facts. However, it is impossible to quote all the times that this "muddling of tracks" has occurred in Fulcanelli's story. It must suffice to know that it exists and consequently, to be on one's guard.

During the last years of his life, Eugène Canseliet told many an anecdote, which were quoted in either Jacques Chancel's *Radioscopie*[276], the periodical *La Tourbe des Philosophes*, or in *Le Feu du Soleil*. We will now quote a few of them for the reader:

Eugène Canseliet wrote that in 1871, the year of the Commune Insurrection, the man who would come to be known as Fulcanelli participated in the defence of Paris under the command of the famous architect, Viollet-le-Duc, then a lieutenant-colonel.

This is quite correct, and it should also be mentioned that it was Marcellin Berthelot who chaired the Scientific Committee for the Defence of Paris, in which participated the youthful Jules Violle, who had shortly prior to this defended his thesis at the Sorbonne. Edouard Branly, who had become a friend when they were both studying at Ecole Normale Supérieure, was also a member of this committee. Thanks to this long-standing friendship, they periodically met; for example, when they attended with their friend, Prosper Plein, "lectures on the threats to Christianity". Let us recall the synopsis of *Finis Gloriae Mundi*: did it not mention "religious disbelief" as a major factor contributing to the "decline of our civilization"?

In his *Alchimiques Mémoires* (*La Tourbe des Philosophes*), quoted from his diary, Eugène Canseliet wrote for October 10, 1921:

---

[276] A French radio programme (Tr.).

We had the coveted happiness to prematurely admire, near our master's furnace, this glass through which we - the moved and enthusiastic spectator – observed the slow succession of the imperceptible shades of the philosophical prism. From the substance issued from the salt delivered by the black caput on that liquefied substance, gradually heated to an adequate degree, Fulcanelli took up a small quantity of the precious enamel on a rod, which was easily detached from its steel support after cooling down. There resides the secret of glass coloured in the mass in Middle-Ages stained-glass windows, for which it was essential that the pieces be set in the purest lead.

This text is extremely important for it illustrates the colours produced in the alchemical Egg during its coction. It also raises the issue of producing the blue and red seen in the stained-glass windows of Chartres cathedral, which preoccupied Jean-Julien Champagne and René Schwaller de Lubicz so much, as we mentioned in a previous section.

There is another fact of some significance, mentioned by Eugène Canseliet in the interview he granted to the magazine *Le Grand Albert*:

> As far as separation is concerned, I also happened to achieve a successful, perfect one in my garret room on quai des Célestins, witnessed by Mohtar Pasha. One has to have the knack: one very sharp blow with the hammer. Mohtar Pasha was dazzled and flabbergasted, and wanted to take me to Egypt.

And in his *Alchimiques Mémoires*:

> At the end of the summer of 1932, when I became acquainted and formed a friendship with the husband of HH Princess Nimet, sister of king Fuad I of Egypt, i.e., with General Mahmud Mohtar Pasha...

And about Fulcanelli:

> I can say now that I never doubted that the affectionate and brotherly attention showed to me by Mohtar Pasha was in any way the consequence of subtle luck. And I am certain that he was acquainted with Fulcanelli and, even further, with his surname; that is to say, the legal designation of his person in any place in France. [...] And undoubtedly he [*Fulcanelli*] had also known Mahmud Mohtar Pasha.

In his *Alchimiques Mémoires*, Eugène Canseliet also referred to the friendly relationship between Fulcanelli and Anatole France:

> The facts go back to 1920, when having left Cap d'Antibes and returned to his princely home, Villa Saïd, Anatole France came to greet and hug his old comrade of the days of old. As for Fulcanelli, he made grave remarks to Jérôme Coignard regarding his health, which arose in him a legitimate anxiousness.

Jean-Julien Champagne was also acquainted with Anatole France, whom he probably met at the de Lessepses:

> He [*Anatole France*] feared the presence of Champagne, who never took long before smoking a cigarette, and who dragged behind him the persistent smell of tobacco. It is true that Fulcanelli, although he *never smoked*, found that keen sense of smell rather excessive. (*E. Canseliet was thus obviously differentiating Fulcanelli from J. Champagne here.*)

Eugène Canseliet even alluded to the national funeral of the great writer on October 18, 1924, which he attended, allegedly with Fulcanelli:

> I went there with Fulcanelli who, upset by the long and cruel agony of his old comrade, had wanted me to accompany him.[277]

How can this be when Canseliet says elsewhere that he had not seen Fulcanelli since the previous year? We must simply consider the fact that nobody is alive today that could bear witness to this! How not to forgive these legitimate precautions of the disciple who thus protected the anonymity of the prestigious being with whom he had pledged his word to keep his identity forever unknown to the uninitiated?

\*   \*

\*

Surrounded by his wife, Germaine, and his three daughters - Solange, Béatrice, and Isabelle, Eugène Canseliet passed away in his philosophical dwelling in Savignies, on April 17, 1982. As to the provisions in his will, including the codicil at the end of the reprint

---

[277] *Alchimiques Mémoires*, no.s 1516, p. 12.

of his *Deux Logis Alchimiques* (1979), they could not be carried out because *his precious diary mysteriously disappeared shortly after his demise.* He had written:

> This is a mine in which Isabelle, my second daughter, will be allowed to dig as much as she wants, after the time has come for me to disappear. Thus, she will have some resources made available by J. J. Pauvert for whom the collection of all these souvenirs is intended, and this is justice.[278]

I, myself, would like to pay a last tribute to that unique man, my good master of Savignies, by giving an excerpt of the text I published shortly after his passing:

> How many among those who, in the neighbourhood of Notre-Dame, in the hermetic vicinity of Saint-Séverin, at the corner of rue de la Huchette, have come across a little man, aged, certainly, but with intensely acute and sharp eyes, impeccably dressed, carrying a big shoulder-strap bag, and have suddenly felt this strange breath that *Philosophy* so willingly transmits to *"the children of sapience"*... That man, out of Time, but not in love with a remote past - as his detractors used to assert - always bore the image of the perfect Philosopher "on the fringe of Science and History", whose "charitable" work will perpetuate beyond the years . . . .[279]

He went away on a beautiful spring day, but thanks to his considerable work, the memory of Fulcanelli will remain forever . . . . immortal!

---

[278] *La Tourbe des Philosophes*, no.3, p.15.
[279] *Atlantis*, no. 322, Sept.-Oct. 1982.

# Appendix

# Letter addressed to Fulcanelli's "initiator" after his access to adeptship

(Excerpt from Eugène Canseliet's second preface to *Le Mystère des Cathédrales*, 1957)

[...] *At that time, we were unaware of the deeply moving letter, which we shall reproduce a little further on, and which owes its amazing beauty to the warm enthusiasm and fervent expression of the writer. Both writer and recipient remain anonymous due to the absence of both the signature and superscription, although the recipient was undoubtedly Fulcanelli's master. Fulcanelli left this revealing letter among his own papers. It has two brown creases where it was folded as a result of having been kept for a long time in his wallet, which did not, however, protect it from the fine, greasy dust of the furnace that was in continual use. So, for many years, the author of* Le Mystère des Cathédrales *kept as a talisman the written proof of his true initiator's triumph, which nothing now prevents us from publishing, particularly since it provides us with a powerful and accurate idea of the sublime domain in which the Great Work takes place. We do not think anyone will object to the length of this strange epistle, from which it would certainly be a pity to remove even one single word:*

My Old Friend,

This time you have truly received the *Gift of God*. It is an amazing Grace, and for the first time I understand how rare this favour is. Indeed, I believe that, in its unfathomable depth of simplicity, the arcanum cannot be found by the strength of reason alone, however subtle and experienced it may be. At last, you possess the *Treasure of Treasures*. Let us give thanks to the Divine

Light that made you a participant in it. Moreover, you have richly deserved it on account of your unwavering belief in Truth, your constancy of effort, your perseverance in sacrifice and also, let us not forget .... *your charitable work.*

When my wife told me the good news, I was stunned with joy and surprise, and my happiness was beyond words. So much so that I said to myself: let us hope we shall not have to pay for this thrilling hour with some terrible aftermath. But, although I was only briefly informed of the event, I believed that I understood it, and what confirms me in my certainty is that *the fire extinguishes only when the Work is accomplished and the entire tinctorial mass impregnates the glass, which, from decantation to decantation, remains absolutely saturated and becomes luminous like the sun.*

You have extended generosity by associating us with this high and occult knowledge, to which you have full right, and which is entirely your own. We, better than any others, can appreciate its worth, and we, more than any others, are capable of being eternally grateful to you for it. You know that the most beautiful phrases, the most eloquent protestations, are not worth as much as the moving simplicity of this single sentence: *you are good*; and it is for this great virtue that God has crowned you with the diadem of true kingship. He knows you will make noble use of the sceptre and of the priceless endowment which it provides. We have known you for a long time as the blue cloak of your friends in need. This charitable cloak has suddenly grown larger, and your noble shoulders are now covered by the azure of the whole sky and its great sun. May you long enjoy this great and rare good fortune, to the joy and consolation of your friends, and even of your enemies, for misfortune cancels out everything. From now on, you will have at your disposal the magic wand, which works all miracles.

My wife, with the unexplicable intuition of sensitive beings, had a very strange dream. She saw a man who was enveloped by all the colours of the rainbow and who ascended up to the Sun. Her explanation was quickly forthcoming. What a miracle! What a beautiful and triumphant reply to my letter, so crammed with arguments and – theoretically - correct, but yet how far from the *Truth, from Reality!* Ah! One can almost say that he who has greeted the *morning star* has forever lost the use of his sight and his reason, for he is fascinated by that false light and cast into the abyss.... Unless, as in your case, a great stroke of fate comes to suddenly pull him away from the edge of the precipice.

I am longing to see you, my Old Friend, to hear you tell me about the last hours of anguish and triumph. But be assured that I will never be able to express in words the great joy that we feel and all the gratitude we have at the bottom of our hearts. Hallelujah!

I give you a hug and congratulate you.

Your Old ......."

He who knows how to achieve the Work *by the one and only mercury* has found that which is most perfect - that is to say, he has received the Light and achieved the Magisterium.

# Bibliography

AMADOU Robert, *Le Feu du Soleil, Entretien sur l'alchimie avec Eugène Canseliet*, J.J Pauvert, Paris, 1978.

AMBELAIN Robert, *Dossier Fulcanelli*, Bibliothèque Nationale.

CANSELIET Eugène,
- *Alchimie*, J. J. Pauvert, Paris, 1964.
- *L'Alchimie et son livre muet Mutus Liber*, J. J. Pauvert, Paris, 1967.
- *L'Alchimie expliquée sur ses textes classiques*, publisher: J. J. Pauvert, Paris, 1972.
- *Trois anciens Traités d'Alchimie*, J. J. Pauvert, Paris, 1975.
- *Les deux Logis alchimiques*, reprint J. J. Pauvert, Paris, 1979. (First edition: Jean Schemit, Paris, 1945)
- Numerous articles published in the following periodicals: *Atlantis, Les Cahiers d'Hermès, La Tour Saint-Jacques, Initiation et Science, La Tourbe des Philosophes*.
Also numerous forewords for various authors; *Etude historique sur Nicolas Flamel*, publisher: Denoël, coll. "Bibliotheca Hermetica", Paris 1977; article inserted in *L'Alchimie* by E. J. Holmyard, publisher: Arthaud, Paris, 1979; article in *L'Art magique* by André Breton, "Formes et Reflets", Paris, 1957. For biographical details, please see, *La Tourbe des Philosophes,* as well as the Internet site, http://www.alchymie.net

COURJEAUD Frédéric, *Fulcanelli: Une identité révélée*, publisher: Claire Vigne, Paris, 1996.

DUBOIS Geneviève, *Fulcanelli dévoilé*, publisher: Dervy, Paris, 1992.

FULCANELLI,
- *Le Mystère des Cathédrales*, reprint J. J. Pauvert, Paris.
- *Les Demeures philosophales*, reprint J. J. Pauvert, Paris. First published by Jean Schemit, then by *L'Omnium Littéraire*; successive prefaces by Eugène Canseliet.

KHAITZINE Richard, *Fulcanelli et le Cabaret du Chat noir*, publisher: Ramuel, 1997, in collaboration with Johan DREUE, CD-ROM, Archimed Diffusion.

LAPLACE Jean,
- *Révélations alchimiques sur la Fin du Monde*, publisher: Editions de la Tourbe, Grenoble, 1978.
- *Index général des Termes spéciaux, des Expressions et des Sentences propres à l'Alchimie, se rencontrant dans l'Oeuvre complète d'Eugène Canseliet*, publisher: Suger, Paris, 1986.
- Articles in *La Tourbe des Philosophes*.

MARTINEZ OTERO Luis-Miguel, *Fulcanelli, une Biographie impossible*, publisher: Arista, 1989.

PAUWELS Louis and BERGIER Jacques, *Le Matin des Magiciens*, publisher: Gallimard, 1960.

RAYNER JOHNSON Kenneth, *The Fulcanelli Phenomenon*, publisher: Neville Spearman, Jersey, 1980.

RIVIERE Patrick,
- *Alchimie et Spagyrie, du Grand Oeuvre à la Médecine de Paracelse*, publisher: éditions de Neustrie, 1986.
- *Alchimie: Science et Mystique*, publisher: De Vecchi, Paris, reprint 2000.
- *Saint-Germain et Cagliostro et les Mystères Rose-Croix*, publisher: De Vecchi, Paris.
- *Le Graal: Histoire et Symboles*, publisher: Le Rocher, Paris.
- *Alchimie & Archimie: l'Art des Particuliers ou des Teintures auriques ...*, publisher: éditions du Cosmogone, 2002.

- CD-ROM: *Le Grand Oeuvre par Voie sèche selon les préceptes de Fulcanelli et d'E. Canseliet*, publisher: Arcadis, 2004.
- *Internet site*: http://www.alchymie.net